PDB Me to Oracle Cloud

Zero Downtime Migration To Oracle Cloud

Pocket Solutions Guide

PDB Me to Oracle Cloud
Pocket Solutions Guide

Real-Life Solutions for the Cloud

Charles Kim @racdba

Jim Czuprynski @jimthewhyguy

Pini Dibask @pini_dibask

Cloud and Multitenant Experts
Oracle OpenWorld 2019 Edition
http://ViscosityNA.com

ISBN-13:   978-1977809643

ISBN-10: 1977809642

About Viscosity

Known as "Trusted Advisors", Experts in Oracle Cloud, RAC, Exadata, Virtualization, Big Data, & Cloud

Viscosity North America (http://viscosityna.com) is a recognized premier consulting firm of database technologies, cloud, and application development. Viscosity was founded by industry and authored experts. Many of our experts, are prominent thought leaders with extensive backgrounds in Oracle databases, performance tuning, and virtualization.

Viscosity was formed by former Oracle employees, each of which worked in various capacities within the Oracle Corporation. These capacities include Oracle Database, RAC Development, Oracle Consulting, Oracle Technical Architects, as well as Design and Performance Tuning experts. Viscosity's Oracle Center of Expertise has developed best practices and tight partner relationships to implement world-class solutions. Our vast experience and intellectual property give customers insight into what is driving IT complexity. We can deliver a set of practical executable plans for simplifying IT infrastructure, helping reduce operating costs, while freeing up resources for new business initiatives.

For your enterprise and commercial software and solution needs, Viscosity will custom build software to serve your business, integrate and extend your purchased enterprise apps, or update your legacy and dated solutions with usability and security. Need it on any cloud or mobile platform? No problem.

Viscosity Services Include
- Cloud Migrations
  - Cloud Assessments
  - Hybrid Cloud
- Exadata
  - Exadata Installation and Configuration
  - Exadata Patching and Upgrades
  - Exadata Migration
  - Exadata Managed Services
  - Exadata Consolidation
- Application Development
  - Custom Development
  - Cloud & Mobile Development
- Real Application Clusters (RAC) Implementation and Tuning
- Disaster Recovery Planning and Data Guard Implementation
- SharePlex Zero Downtime Database Upgrades / Migrations
- GoldenGate Implementation
- Database Performance Tuning
  - Performance Assessment
  - Proactive Assessment
- Database Managed Services
- Database Upgrades to Oracle Database 12c & 11g Release 2 with Zero Downtime
- E-Business Suite Administration and Upgrades
  - E-Business Suite Managed Services
- Peoplesoft Upgrades and Administration
  - Peoplesoft Managed Services
- Data Warehousing Implemenation and Design

- Big Data Infrastructure Support (Cloudera with Hadoop and NoSQL)
- Enterprise Application Development
- Oracle License Optimization

Contact us at info@viscosityna.com for additional details on how we can help solve your performance problems, mitigate risk or even perform a proactive assessment of your database environment.

DEDICATION

Charles Kim

This book is dedicated to my three boys:
Isaiah, Jeremiah, and Noah.

Jim Czuprynski

To my father, James Czuprynski Sr., for his constant insistence that I should "always use the right tool for the right job, dammit!" and his reminders to "let the tool do the work, fer crissakes." Not a day passes without me missing his terrible jokes, his stern but loving advice, and the sacrifices he made for me and our family. *Dobranoc i dziękuję*, Dad.

Pini Dibask

This book is dedicated to my beloved parents, Ruth and Zeev, for their endless support and encouragement.

TABLE OF CONTENTS

PDB Me to Oracle Cloud 1

Zero Downtime Migration To Oracle Cloud 1

Pocket Solutions Guide 1

PDB Me to Oracle Cloud 2

Pocket Solutions Guide 2
    About Viscosity 5

DEDICATION 7
    Charles Kim 7
    Jim Czuprynski 7
    Pini Dibask 7

Preface 12

ACKNOWLEDGMENTS 14
    Charles Kim 14
    Jim Czuprynski 14
    Pini Dibask 14

Additional Books by the Authors 15

1.   The *Dao* of Oracle Public Cloud 17
    What Does Cloud Hold for Oracle DBAs? 17
    Why Oracle Public Cloud? 17

2.   Establishing a DBaaS OPC Environment 20
    Allocating a DBaaS Subscription 20
    Establishing an OPC DBaaS Environment 24
    Controlling a DBaaS Service Instance Via the Cloud Service Console ... 35
    Connecting to an OPC DBaaS Environment via Terminal Emulator 37
        Generating a PuTTY PPK File with PuTTYGen 37
        Connecting to Your DBaaS Environment Via PuTTY 42

3.   Constructing and Managing Databases in OPC DBaaS 49
    Removing the Existing CDB 49
    Building New CDBs 49
    Setting Up Security Keystores 52
    Building New PDBs for Feature Demonstration 57
    Confirming Successful PDB Setup 70
    Completing Network Connectivity for PDBs 71
    Creating Security Keystore for CDB2 73
    Enabling a Keystore for AUTOLOGIN 74
    Disabling and Re-Enabling AUTOLOGIN Mode 75

5.   Leveraging Oracle Public Cloud DBaaS REST API 78
    Viewing Instance Status 78
    Creating an Instance 79
    Controlling Domain Instances 79

6.   **PDB Migration and Refreshes** **82**
   PDB "Hot" Migration **83**
   Leveraging Refreshable PDBs **94**
   Leveraging Proxy PDBs **102**
     Dictionary Views 103

7.   **DBaaS Backup and Recovery** **106**
   PDB Level RMAN Backup **107**
   PDB Recovery After Loss of a Datafile **108**
   Restoring a Pluggable Database from RMAN Backup **109**
     Point-In-Time Recovery of the PDB based on SCN 110
   Recover a Dropped Pluggable Database **114**
   Flashing Back a Single PDB **114**

8.   **Winning Performance Challenging in Oracle Multitenant** **121**
   Introduction to this Chapter **121**
   Ensuring High Quality of Service (QoS) **121**
     Oracle 12c Release 1 122
     Oracle 12c Release 2 and Above 124
   Performance Monitoring when Using Oracle Multitenant **125**
     Dictionary Views 125
     AWR 126
     Monitoring Tools 126
     Multi-Dimensional Analysis 128
     Baselining 130
     Compare 130
     Change Tracking 131
   Chapter Summary **131**

9.   **Resource Control and Governance** **133**
   Implementing PDB Resource Governance **137**
     Limiting IO On the CDB (Throttling Across Every PDB) 138
     Limiting I/O on a Specific PDB 138
     Throttling Memory Limits for a PDB 139
   Utilizing PDB-Level Heat Maps, Information Lifecycle Management (ILM), and
   Automatic Data Optimization (ADO) **140**

10.   **Appendices** **154**
   Fundamentals of PDBs That Every DBA Needs to Know **154**
     Connecting to a CDB or root container (CDB$ROOT) 154
     Connect to the PDB Using Easy Connect Method 154
   Connecting to a PDB Using TNS **155**
     Connecting Directly to PBD Using TWO_TASK 155
     Starting and Shutting Down CDBs and PDBs 156
     Executing a Script Across Multiple Pluggable Databases 157
     Manipulating the SQL Prompt to Display the Current PDB 157
     glogin.sql 157
     Switch_cont.sql ($ORACLE_HOME/sqlplus/admin directory) 158
     Enforcing a PDB's Saved State 158
   Additional Helpful PDB Scripts **161**
   PROD_AP Schema Population Scripts **163**

ABOUT THE AUTHORS **174**
   Charles Kim **174**

Jim Czuprynski...175
Pini Dibask..175

Preface

As Cloud Computing has evolved and matured, it has sparked growing interest from the enterprise market where economic pressures are challenging traditional IT operations. Many companies and government agencies are being faced with growing IT costs that originate from multiple sources such as legacy systems, software licensing, power consumption, and operating overhead. These growing costs are exacerbated by the inefficiencies in traditional IT organizations such as project-based funding, underutilization of resources, lengthy manual provisioning times, and organizational silos. Cloud Computing, either through Private or Public cloud initiatives, is focused on addressing these issues by reducing costs through better standardization, higher utilization, greater agility, and faster responsiveness of IT services.

However, a high-priority concern for many enterprises in embarking on a private, public, or hybrid cloud journey is the security of the infrastructure as well as the information stored and processed by that infrastructure. This is particularly important for firms in domains with a high level of regulation and/or sensitive customer data. Balancing rich mechanisms for identity and access management with integral features such as single sign-on is a must for cloud environments.

Securing information and software assets in the cloud can be problematic, especially in public cloud environments where the systems are not directly controlled by the data owners. However, the same principles and lessons learned in developing the on-premise Private Cloud solutions can also be applied to Public Cloud ideology.

The outcome from the IOUG 2016 Survey on Database Cloud revealed that security and privacy concerns are highest on the list of challenges for cloud adoption. Despite security concerns, enterprises are increasing their footprint in the cloud each year. The public cloud has become a dominant force that is shaking up how companies do business today and has become a disruptive technology.

For the past 5 years, RightScale (RightScale.com) has conducted an annual State of the Cloud Survey of the latest cloud computing trends with 1,060 IT professionals, of which 42% of the respondents represented companies with over 1,000 employees. With a focus on Infrastructure as a Service (IaaS), they reported that hybrid cloud adoption increased from 58% the previous year to 71% in 2016. Hybrid cloud adoption also increased as a direct result of private cloud adoption, increasing to 77% from 63% the previous year. They also reported that over 17% of the enterprises have over 1,000 VMs in the cloud.

If you are not already in the Cloud, you need to assess which of the three components - Infrastructure as a Service (IaaS), Platform as a Service (PaaS), and Software as a Service (SaaS) - you want to migrate, and which of the three public Cloud computing components you need: Iaas, PaaS, or SaaS. You may come to the conclusion that all you need is just one component, a combination, or all three of the components.

If you are starting a new application development project, consider the Cloud as a potential platform of choice. Instead of pricing out storage and compute servers for development projects, you should also look at the cost of doing business in the Cloud. In determining cost associated with standing up new hardware, installing operating systems, application servers, and databases, factor in the operational expenses (OPEX) in addition to the capital expenses (CAPEX). When OPEX is factored into the cost of building your own infrastructure, the Cloud becomes significantly easier to justify.

Management of resources in the cloud provides a significant opportunity for cost savings, such as shutting down unused workloads, selecting lower-cost Cloud options, or placement of resources within cheaper regions. Cost management includes optimization actions to monitor utilization and rightsizing instances as needed on a regular basis. The concept of metered and non-metered environments is available for enterprises to choose from.

The Public Cloud becomes faster and better with each passing year. With that in mind, vendors for the public cloud are investing more and more in infrastructure (compute, network and storage) compelling customers to place more resources into their cloud. Customers traditionally perceive cloud to be slow, and that the Cloud will never be able to meet their IO and compute requirements. However, Cloud vendors are delivering faster VMs and options for flash and solid state disks, enabling Cloud vendors to offer additional options for SLAs, dedicated resources, and virtual private networks.

Many customers have a need to instantiate an environment on demand and to shrink their footprint as needed. As projects start to ramp up, typically additional compute and storage resources are needed. If the initial project infrastructure started in the Cloud, the Cloud provides agility and scalability to easily expand the infrastructure footprint in the cloud. As projects start to wind down and less demand is required for compute and storage, shrinking your investment in the Cloud is extremely easy. The dynamic on-demand expansion and contraction of compute and storage resources can enable projects to be effective and even finish under budget.

ACKNOWLEDGMENTS

Charles Kim

Many thanks to my co-author for always striving for excellence and trying to make this book better each month.

I would like to extend a personal thanks to Kelsie Brunson for helping proof edit this book! We couldn't have made the tight deadlines without you.

Jim Czuprynski

I'd like to thank the technical team at Viscosity NA - especially Charles Kim and David Knight - for their teamwork as we set up a robust OPC DBaaS environment that enabled the voluminous research and tedious experimentation to perfect our understanding of how best to handle all things multitenant in Oracle Database 12cR2, including how keystores work to preserve tight security for OPC DBaaS.

Pini Dibask

I'd like to thank my Manager, Venkat Rajaji, for his trust, support and guidance throughout my ongoing journey in Product Management at Quest Software.

Also, I'd like to thank the Viscosity Team, Charles Kim and Monica Li, for the opportunity to participate in writing this book which covers the most exciting Oracle database technology in the last decade – the Oracle Multitenant option.

Additional Books by the Authors

Viscosity evangelists have written over 17 books in total, on Oracle and the various emerging technologies that surround Oracle.

Jim Czuprynski has co-authored three books on Oracle database technology focusing primarily on techniques and tools that every Oracle DBA can leverage during his/her day-to-day, normal (or not-so-normal!) administration tasks.

1. The *Dao* of Oracle Public Cloud

If you are an Oracle DBA who's looking to finally take the leap into Cloud technology, this chapter will help you understand what Cloud is all about and why it's crucial for your career to make the transition to this brave new world of computing – essentially, to absorb the *dao* (or path) of Cloud and what that trajectory means for your future.

What Does Cloud Hold for Oracle DBAs?

The concept of Cloud computing is actually quite simple, as many Oracle DBAs have already been pursuing this path for some time, albeit in a somewhat disjointed fashion. Consider the typical, non-cloud siloed environment that most organizations still employ: There are separate domains dedicated for computing (application and database servers) as well as storage (NAS, NFS, or SAN) and networking bandwidth.

What's typically missing in these siloed environments is the ability to quickly and easily ramp up or ramp down the appropriate storage or compute resources to the application workloads that need those resources in a sufficiently flexible manner. While virtualization has certainly progressed dramatically in the last decade – expanding to storage and even networking (as part of software-defined networks) – a siloed environment still prevents efficient, effective *orchestration* of these resources.

A final driving force behind Cloud adoption is the onset of application development practices, like DevOps and Agile that demand extreme rapid deployment of applications. Gone are the days of "waterfall" project management that typically started with well-defined business requirements, proceeding to detailed requirements, and the expectation that developers wait for a detailed design document, before a single line of code is written. In fact, many businesses now need to implement customer-facing applications within a matter of months or weeks; with many of these applications being discarded shortly after the business need – say, the launch of a new product – has been accomplished. These intense demands mean that in the future, Oracle DBAs will need to be able to spin up a fully-populated development database within *minutes*, not days.

Why Oracle Public Cloud?

While there are many Cloud computing environments already available – for example, Microsoft Azure or Amazon Web Services (AWS) Relational Database Service (RDS) – the Oracle Public Cloud (OPC) is a compelling environment to consider for several reasons.

- First and foremost, Oracle has designed and built OPC as a second-generation cloud platform. Put simply, it's been designed upon the bones of the mistakes of the first generation of other cloud providers.

- OPC runs on Oracle's hardware, uses its own OS (Oracle Enterprise Linux or Solaris), leverages the efficiencies of Oracle Virtual Machine, and (depending on the database release selected) makes available database features within different tiers of pricing. If a developer doesn't need to leverage, say, partitioning, it's a simple matter to spin up an SE2 Edition of an Oracle Database versus an "extreme" version of Enterprise Edition that features Database In-Memory, Multitenancy, and other advanced features. In other words, OPC is specifically designed to run Oracle databases and corresponding database applications better than any other home-grown environment.

- Though we are focused on OPC in this book, be aware that Oracle does offer its own Private Cloud option as well, available in several different configurations and support schemes depending on where your organization needs or wants to place its servers and storage and how much involvement is desired for management of that hardware and environment. Either way, the Oracle Private Cloud is still elementally Oracle Cloud – it is the same software and hardware that the Oracle Public Cloud is running. And that means a true hybrid cloud solution is really only available through Oracle Cloud.

- Lastly, be aware that Oracle "eats its own cooking": All of Oracle Corporation's internal business processes run within its Cloud. This makes it uniquely positioned as a proving ground for the databases and applications it's customer base already uses.

2. Establishing a DBaaS OPC Environment

Before you build a DBaaS OPC environment, you'll need to obtain Cloud credits. Your organization may have already purchased these credits, or may even have been granted a considerable amount of credits during a recent software or hardware license renewal, so be sure to check with your current OPC administration team before considering the purchase of additional credits.

Allocating a DBaaS Subscription

If your organization hasn't purchased or been granted OPC credits, there's a simple way to begin your journey to the Oracle Public Cloud: purchasing a small number of credits directly from the Oracle Store website (https://shop.oracle.com).

Note: As this book goes to press, Oracle Corporation continues to offer $300 in free OPC credits. Also, note that a valid e-mail address, an Oracle SSO account, and valid credit card number are required to sign up for these Cloud credits. Finally, this offer may be withdrawn at some point in the future or replaced by another offer. Please be sure you understand the implications of signing up for any such offer, especially the conditions under which you could continue to be billed for Cloud services after the trial period elapses.

To purchase sufficient OPC credits, simply navigate your browser to the Oracle Store and begin the acquisition process as shown in **Figure 1**.

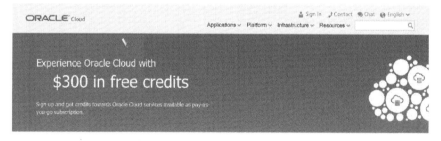

Figure 1. Oracle Cloud Subscription: Introductory Free Cloud Credits

Clicking on the **Get started for free** button takes you to a simple sign-up form (**Figure 2**).

Figure 2. Oracle Cloud Subscription: Sign-Up Instructions

Click the **Sign up** button to proceed to the Oracle Single Sign-on (SSO) Account creation form (**Figure 3**). Note that if you already have an existing Oracle SSO account, you can bypass this form by clicking on the **Sign In** link.

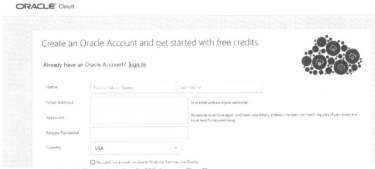

Figure 3. Oracle Cloud Subscription: Oracle SSO Account Sign-Up

Next, it's time to connect with your Oracle SSO account credentials, as shown in **Figure 4**.

*If the SSO account you've specified has **already** been associated with past free Cloud credit offers, the web site will eventually reject your subsequent requests for more free credits.*

Figure 4. Oracle Cloud Subscription: Single Sign-On (SSO) Prompt

Click the *Sign In* button to proceed to add your payment details, as shown in **Figure 5**.

Oracle Cloud Sign Up

*US$300 in free credits included. Valid for 30 days.

Verification

Please confirm your mobile number by requesting and providing the verification code.

Country Code	Mobile Number	
(+1) United States		Request Code

Verification Code	
	⊘ Verified

A verification code will be sent in a text message to your phone. Standard text messaging rates apply. Oracle may also

Use Account Details	
Yes	∨

You may see two temporary charges of $1 each on your payment method. These are verification holds which will be removed automatically, typically within 3 to 5 days. **Your payment method will not be charged unless you opt in to convert to Pay As You Go and exceed the free credit amount.** See FAQ for more details.

You will be redirected automatically to another page to enter your payment method details. Oracle uses the secure third-party payment processor CyberSource for payment processing. Please refer to CyberSource's privacy statement for the terms applicable to the data collected.

Figure 5. Oracle Cloud Subscription: Acknowledgment

*If you've specified a **different** Oracle SSO account, but have already used the **same** credit card number to sign up for free Cloud credits, your subsequent request will likely be rejected.*

Once you've supplied an acceptable payment method, you'll receive an e-mail with details on how to sign in and proceed with establishing your new OPC DBaaS environment.

Establishing an OPC DBaaS Environment

Now that you've secured sufficient OPC credits, it's time to build your first OPC-resident Oracle database.

After you've received an e-mail acknowledging your successful procurement of OPC credits, your first step is to access your account using the information provided within.

Supply the proper values for the Account Type – in this case, choose **Traditional Cloud Account** - and then supply the OPC datacenter you've been assigned as shown in Figure 61 below. Click on the **My Services** button to proceed.

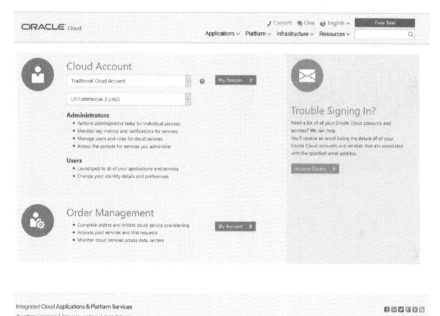

Figure 6. Accessing Your Oracle Cloud Account: Initial screen

Next, supply the Identity Domain you were assigned as shown in **Figure 2** and click the **Go** button.

SIGN IN TO
ORACLE CLOUD

Enter your Identity Domain

a427312

Identity Domain

Go

ORACLE

Figure 7. Choosing your Identity Domain

Next, supply the assigned username and your chosen password, and then click the *Sign In* button to access your account, as **Figure 3** shows.

Figure 8. Accessing your account

Figure 4 shows an example of the OPC Dashboard that you'll use to access your available OPC resources. It contains important governance information as well, including how much of your original Cloud credits remain.

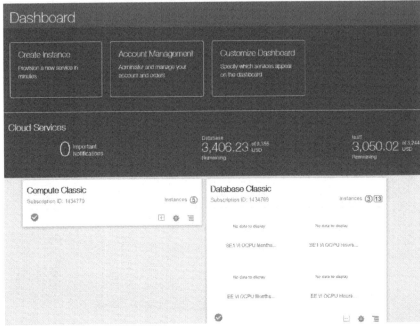

Figure 9. OPC Dashboard

To create a new DBaaS instance, click on the large *Create Instance* button near the left top of the Dashboard. That will offer you the choice of building an instance focused on either Compute, Storage, or Database functionality, as **Figure 5** shows. Choose Database Classic by clicking the *Create* button next to that option.

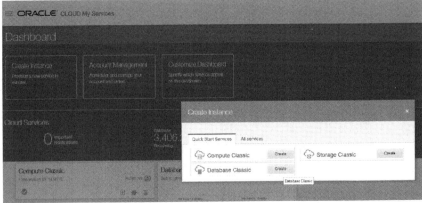

Figure 10. Creating an Instance: Choosing from Quick Start Services

The next step is to create the Database Service that will be hosting your DBaaS database. From the My Services console (**Figure 6**), click the *Create Service* button to start answering questions about your new database.

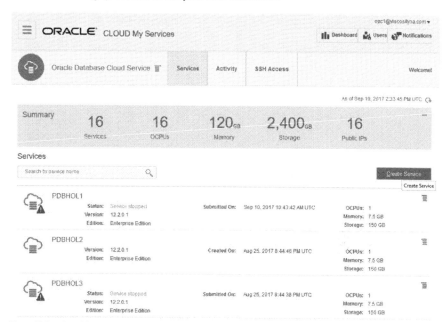

Figure 11. Creating a DBaaS Service Instance: Getting Started

It's time to make some decisions about your Database Service (**Figure 7**):

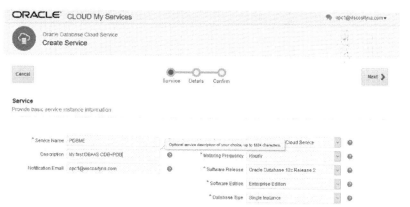

Figure 12. Creating a DBaaS Service Instance: Environmental Decisions

At this point, here's what you're deciding:

- **Service Name** and **Service Description.** Specify a name for your new service instance – we've chosen PDBME – and optionally a short description of the intended usage and contents.
- **Notification Email.** This is the e-mail address to which any notifications of

status changes for the new service instance will be sent. The default is the original e-mail account which was used to request the account, but it can be overridden - so choose wisely to avoid being inundated with unwanted e-mail traffic.

- **Metering Frequency.** This is probably the most crucial choice you can make, so choose wisely:
  - Choosing *Monthly* means that your account will be billed once a month at a fixed cost. This option probably makes the most sense when the instance will be used on a consistent basis – for example, to host a database application that's constantly accessed with minimal spikes of user activity.
  - Likewise, choosing *Hourly* means that your account will only be billed when the instance consumes resources. Therefore, if this instance is going to be used mainly for experimentation or will simply languish at times with significant periods of utter disuse, choosing the Hourly option will likely mean you'll save quite a bit in Cloud credits.
- **Software Release.** You can choose from among several options; since this book is all about the latest release as of this writing, we've selected the 12cR2 release.
- **Software Edition.** Selecting Standard Edition 2 (SE2) will significantly reduce consumption of Cloud credits, but the trade-off is a significant reduction in database features (e.g. partitioning). If you know for certain your applications won't require any of the more advanced capabilities of Enterprise Edition (EE) or any of the other even more robust options (e.g. Extreme Performance), then SE2 is probably a sensible choice. Just remember that once selected, your instance is locked into that edition and cannot be upgraded or downgraded to a different edition.
- **Database Type.** While it's certainly possible to configure a Real Applications Cluster (RAC) -enabled service instance for your database, it will certainly consume more Cloud credits than the standard single-instance database we've selected here.

Once all your choices are complete, simply click the **Next** button to continue to the next configuration steps.

Note: As Oracle continues to improve the breadth of its OPC DBaaS offerings, the price of these OPC options is subject to change in the future. For quick access to the current pricing and sizing options, consult the Oracle Public Cloud pricing page: https://cloud.oracle.com/en_US/database/pricing

Now, it's time to finish configuring the resident Oracle database itself, and again there are a myriad of options to choose from as shown in **Figure 13**:

Figure 13. Creating a DBaaS Service Instance: Configuring Database Options

If you've ever used the Database Configuration Assistant (DBCA) tool to create an Oracle database, most of these options are fairly familiar to you, so we won't dwell on the more obvious choices like DB Name, PDB Name, passwords, storage, and so forth. Nevertheless, there are a few important options to note on this panel:

- o **Compute Shape**. This option determines how many Oracle CPUs (OCPUs) ths service instance requires when it's running.
- o **SSH Public Key**. We'll review how to supply this in just a bit.
- o **Use High Performance Storage**. This option requests that higher performance storage – essentially, flash instead of disk – will be supplied for your service instance's storage needs.

The **Backup and Recovery Configuration** section allows you to choose a backup strategy for your databases within this service instance. Briefly, your three options include **None** (no backups will be taken), **Cloud Only** (one copy of backups is retained), and **Local and Cloud** (two copies of all backups will be retained).

Note: For sake of brevity, we've chosen None, but again – be sure you understand the implications of choosing this option!

Finally, note that it's also possible to initialize a DBaaS service instance's database from an existing set of database backups stored within the Cloud. The ***Initialize from Backup*** section is where we'd specify the location of the backup as well as the source database for those backups.

Next, lets tackle how to connect securely to the new service instance. You most likely have already been assigned an existing private-public key pair for this instance; if so, you can either choose to specify the name of the public key file on the host from which you're going to be accessing this database instance, as **Figure 14** shows. Otherwise, you can also choose to paste in a specific key value instead of accessing the public key via file if you prefer:

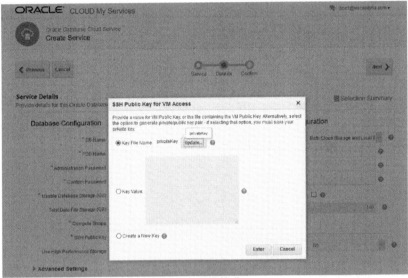

Figure 14. Creating a DBaaS Service Instance: Specifying the SSH Public Key

---

Note: If you haven't received security information from your Cloud administrator, you can generate a new public-private key pair using the **Create a New Key** *option.*

Almost done! After specifying all pertinent options in **Figure 8** and clicking on the **Next** button, you'll get one final chance to confirm your selections, as **Figure 15** shows. Once you're satisfied with your choices, click the **Create** button to initiate the creation of your database service instance.

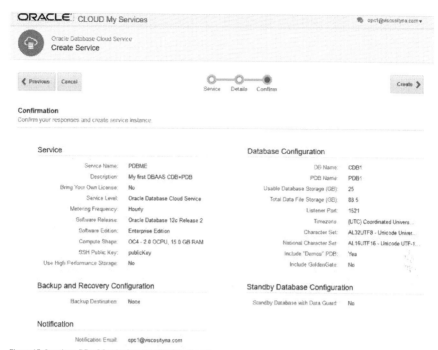

Previous   Cancel   Service   Details   Confirm   Create

Confirmation
Confirm your responses and create service instance

Service

Service Name:	PDBME
Description:	My first DBAAS CDB+PDB
Bring Your Own License:	No
Service Level:	Oracle Database Cloud Service
Metering Frequency:	Hourly
Software Release:	Oracle Database 12c Release 2
Software Edition:	Enterprise Edition
Compute Shape:	OC4 - 2.0 OCPU, 15.0 GB RAM
SSH Public Key:	publicKey
Use High Performance Storage:	No

Database Configuration

DB Name:	CDB1
PDB Name:	PDB1
Usable Database Storage (GB):	25
Total Data File Storage (GB):	83.5
Listener Port:	1521
Timezone:	(UTC) Coordinated Univers...
Character Set:	AL32UTF8 - Unicode Univer...
National Character Set	AL16UTF16 - Unicode UTF-1...
Include "Demos" PDB:	Yes
Include GoldenGate:	No

Backup and Recovery Configuration

Backup Destination:	None

Standby Database Configuration

Standby Database with Data Guard:	No

Notification

Notification Email:	opc1@viscosityna.com

Figure 15. Creating a DBaaS Service Instance: Final Confirmation

We can monitor the progress of the service instance's creation from the My Services Summary page, as shown in **Figure 16**. By clicking on the instance's name (**PDBME**) on that page, we can also access a more detailed view of the instance's creation progress as shown in **Figure 17**.

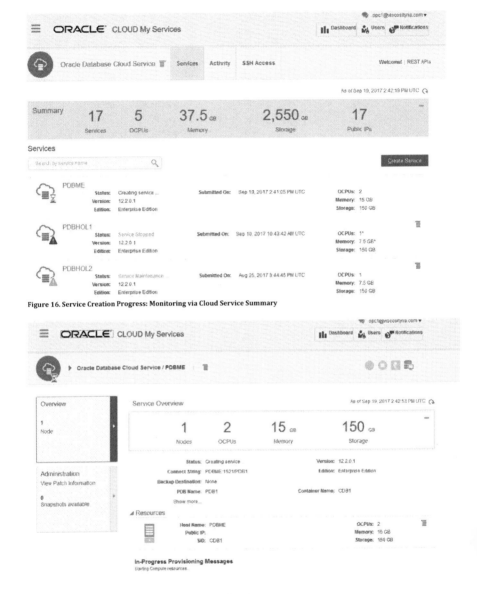

Figure 16. Service Creation Progress: Monitoring via Cloud Service Summary

Figure 17. Service Creation Progress: Monitoring via Service Overview

One other way to monitor the service instance's creation – either while it's in process, or when it's finally completed - is to select the appropriate service from the **Service Create and Delete History** section near the very bottom of the Services Summary page. **Figure 18** below shows the results of the successful creation of the PDBME instance; note that it took approximately 25 minutes for the database instance to complete.

Figure 18. Service Creation Status: Monitoring via Service Create and Delete History

Controlling a DBaaS Service Instance Via the Cloud Service Console

Now that your DBaaS Service Instance has been successfully created, let's take a look at some of the options available for controlling that instance via its Cloud Service Console. Note that there are actually *two* stack menus available on this panel. The bottom stack menu, **Figure 19**, gives you the ability to start, stop, and restart the service instance, as well as upscale or downscale the instance's storage or compute capabilities:

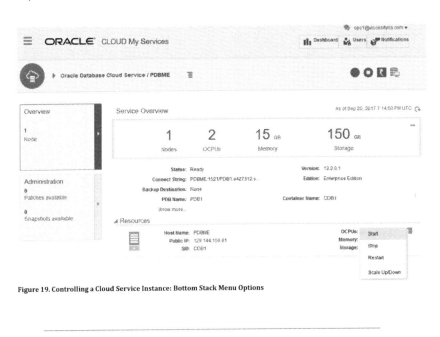

Figure 19. Controlling a Cloud Service Instance: Bottom Stack Menu Options

---

Note: Be aware that upscaling or downscaling a Service Instance does require the instance to be shut down until the expansion or contraction of storage or compute resources is successfully completed.

The second, top-most stack menu, **Figure 20**, includes all of the features of the bottom stack menu plus much more:

- You can open the **DBaaS Monitor** console to look at some basic information about the CDBs and PDBs that reside within the selected service instance.
- The **Application Express** console lets you review what applications you have deployed against your service instance (if any).

- Finally, if it's been enabled for the instance, you can open the **Enterprise Manager (EM)** console to monitor your OPC-based Oracle database.

Note: In the interest of brevity, we won't be covering these different monitoring tools because most Oracle DBAs are already familiar with Oracle Enterprise Manager (OEM).

You can also review the **access rules** for the instance, modify the **SSH access** setup, and view recent **activity** against the service instance.

Figure 20. Controlling a Cloud Service Instance: Top Stack Menu Options

To *start*, *stop*, or *restart* the PDBME instance, you can select from the stack menu near the bottom right of the console panel, as shown in **Figure 20**.

Connecting to an OPC DBaaS Environment via Terminal Emulator

Since most Oracle DBAs are interested in having more than one way to connect to their hosted database environments, we'll next take a look at the steps necessary to connect to your OPC DBaaS service instances using the popular (and free!) PuTTY terminal emulator.

Generating a PuTTY PPK File with PuTTYGen

To keep this simple, we'll leverage the venerable PuTTY utility to access our DBaaS instance. PuTTY has an interesting wrinkle, however: it's necessary to generate a separate *PuTTY private key* (PPK) file via the PuTTYGen utility, downloadable at http://www.putty.org, before accessing DBaaS securely.

Locate the PuTTygen.exe file that you just downloaded and double click on the puttygen.exe executable:

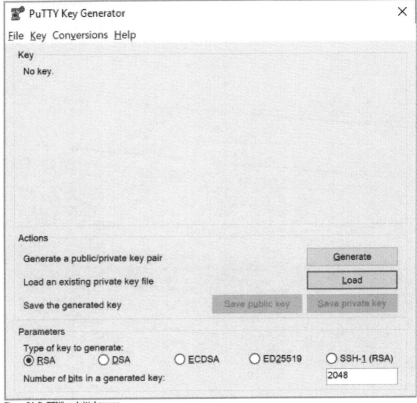

Figure 21. PuTTYGen: Initial screen

Next, click the **Load** button on the Putty Key Generator screen, and then specify the location of the private key you were originally given for these labs, as shown below. Don't forget to choose **All Files (*.*)** from the file types drop down list to allow selection of your SSH private key file. Select the privateKey file and click the **Open** button.

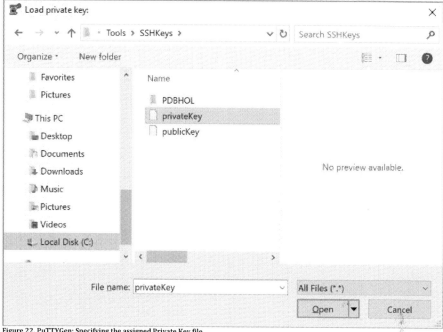

Figure 22. PuTTYGen: Specifying the assigned Private Key file

You should then receive the following confirmation response window. Simply click the OK button to confirm.

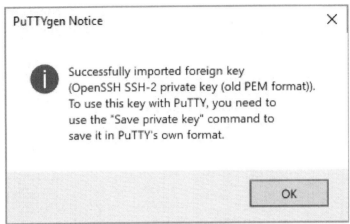

Figure 23. PuTTYGen: Specifying the assigned Private Key file

To save the PPK generated key, click the **Save private key** button.

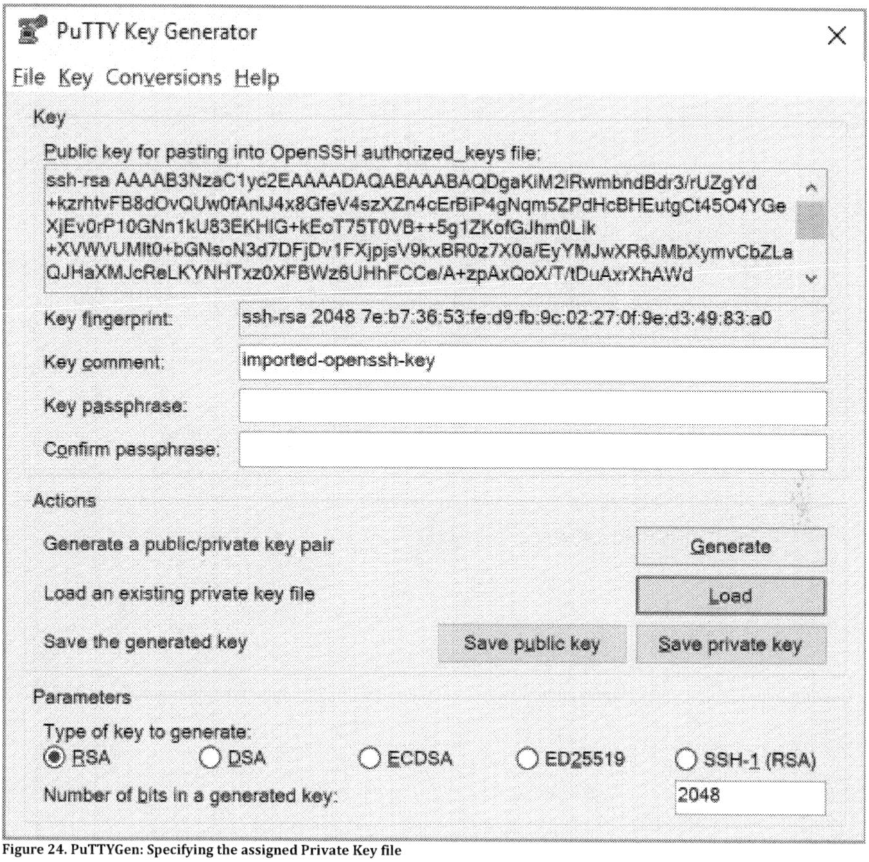

Figure 24. PuTTYGen: Specifying the assigned Private Key file

You'll be reminded that you should save this key with a passphrase, but ignore this reminder by clicking the **Yes** button.

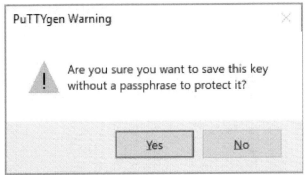

Figure 25. PuTTYGen: Specifying the assigned Private Key file

Save the new private key file with a file name that's appropriate for your PDB lab sessions - perhaps the name of your assigned guest server (in this example, **PDBHOL1**).

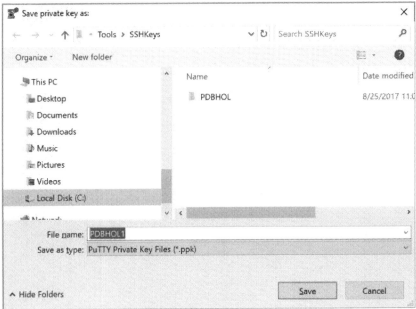

Figure 26. PuTTYGen: Specifying the assigned Private Key file

Connecting to Your DBaaS Environment Via PuTTY

To complete the connection via PuTTY, you will need to locate the public IP address of your personal Oracle Public Cloud DBaaS instance. This information is available via the OPC DBaaS console when you browse the opened Service Instance itself, as shown in **Figure 19** previously.

Connect to your DBaaS instance using the PuTTY terminal emulator (downloadable from http://www.putty.org) to begin the configuration process.

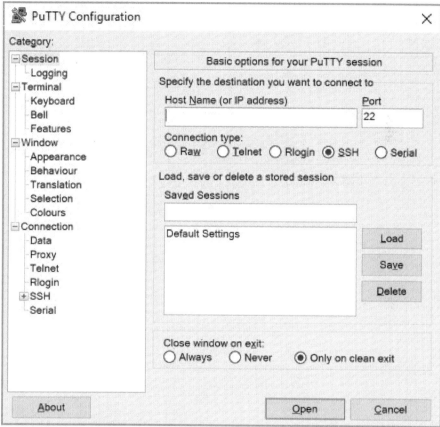

Figure 27. Establishing a PuTTY Terminal Session

We'll first set up SSH authentication. To do that, choose the **SSH ... Auth** option from the left-hand menu.

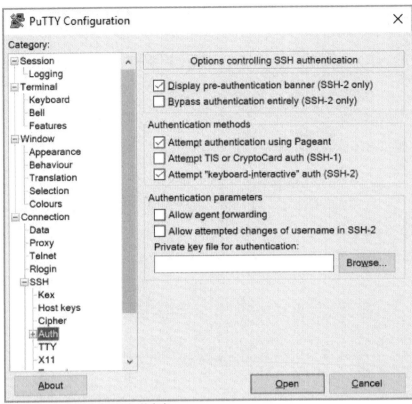

Figure 28. Choosing PuTTY Authentication Methods

Click the **Browse** button to select the location of the supplied PPK file for this course.

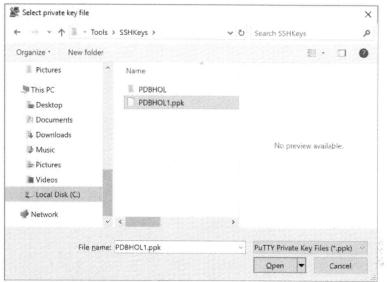

Figure 29. Choosing the assigned PuTTY Private Key (PPK) file

Next, click on **Connection ... Data** in the left-hand menu and then specify **oracle** as the Auto-login username:

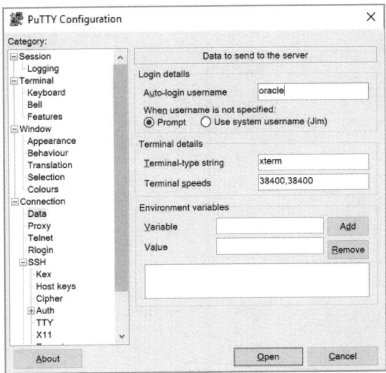

Figure 30. Specifying the Auto-Login User Account

Next, click on *Session* in the left-hand menu and specify the IP address that you have been assigned for the duration of the labs. Note that you can save the PuTTY configuration as well for faster access, as shown below.

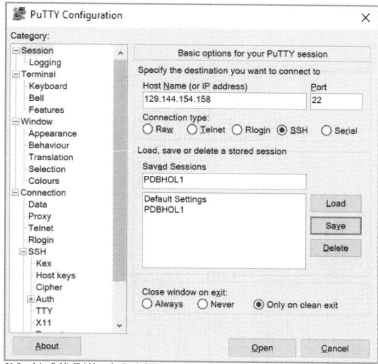

Figure 31. Supplying Public IP Address for Oracle Public Cloud host connection

Click on the **Open** button to attempt to access your assigned host. If this is the first time you've attempted access, you will receive a security warning.

PuTTY Security Alert

⚠ The server's host key is not cached in the registry. You have no guarantee that the server is the computer you think it is.
The server's rsa2 key fingerprint is:
ssh-rsa 2048 61:80:5f:e3:9a:73:7e:23:76:9d:ca:b9:54:3e:d2:01
If you trust this host, hit Yes to add the key to PuTTY's cache and carry on connecting.
If you want to carry on connecting just once, without adding the key to the cache, hit No.
If you do not trust this host, hit Cancel to abandon the connection.

Yes   No   Cancel

Figure 32. Accepting the PuTTY security alert

Simply click on the **Yes** button to accept the key file to PuTTY's cache and continue the connection process. After a few seconds, you should receive a confirmation of a successful connection to your assigned Oracle Public Cloud server, as shown below.

oracle@PDBHOL1:~

```
Using username "oracle".
Authenticating with public key "imported-openssh-key"
[oracle@PDBHOL1 ~]$
```

Figure 33. Successful PuTTY Terminal Session

3. Constructing and Managing Databases in OPC DBaaS

Now that your OPC DBaaS environment is allocated and you've figured out several of the trickier aspects of connecting to it via PuTTY (or any other terminal emulator you prefer!), it's time to delve into how to leverage your environment in the role of traditional Oracle DBA. While it's quite simple to initially configure a DBaaS environment that contains a single CDB and just one PDB, it's actually quite easy to move beyond that basic configuration with Oracle's *Database Configuration Assistant* (DBCA) utility using either its GUI implementation or deploying it via silent installation mode.

To demonstrate, we'll rebuild the entire DBaaS database configuration environment with DBCA, removing the original CDB and its single PDB; replacing with two new CDBs. Along the way, we'll discuss how DBaaS implements its security for a database's tablespaces and what you'll need to know when building CDBs and PDBs in this environment. Through this process you will be able to adopt some subtle tricks to avoid unexpected surprises, especially when creating tablespaces within a new PDB.

Removing the Existing CDB

First, remove the CDB that was originally created as part of building the DBaaS Service instance.

```
$> dbca -silent -deleteDatabase -sourceDB CDB1 -sid CDB1 \
   -sysDBAUserName sys -sysDBAPassword "********"

Connecting to database
4% complete
9% complete
14% complete
19% complete
23% complete
28% complete
47% complete
Updating network configuration files
48% complete
52% complete
Deleting instance and datafiles
76% complete
100% complete
Look at the log file "/u01/app/oracle/cfgtoollogs/dbca/CDB1.log" for
further details.
```

Building New CDBs

Once CDB1 has been successfully removed, you'll rebuild it completely using DBCA to call a response file that builds a new CDB with a single PDB named **PROD_HR**. Here's the invocation of DBCA.

```
$> dbca -silent -createDatabase -responseFile
/home/oracle/CDB1_PROD_HR.rsp
```

Below is the response file used to build CDB1 and its corrsesponding PDB. Note that
the usual comments have been removed from the response file for brevity.

```
################################################################################
## DBCA Response File:  CDB1_PROD_HR.rsp
## Purpose:             Builds a CDB named CDB1 with a single PDB (PROD_HR)
## Author:              Jim Czuprynski
## Maintenance Log:
## 1.0  JSC    Initial version
################################################################################
#-------------------------------------------------------------------------------
# Do not change the following system generated value.
#-------------------------------------------------------------------------------
responseFileVersion=/oracle/assistants/rspfmt_dbca_response_schema_v12.2.0

gdbName=CDB1.compute-a427312.oraclecloud.internal
sid=CDB1
databaseConfigType=SI
policyManaged=false
createServerPool=false
force=false
createAsContainerDatabase=true
numberOfPDBs=1
pdbName=PROD_HR
useLocalUndoForPDBs=true
pdbAdminPassword=********
templateName=/u01/app/oracle/product/12.2.0/dbhome_1/assistants/dbca/templates/General_P
urpose.dbc
sysPassword=*********
systemPassword=**********
emExpressPort=5500
runCVUChecks=false
omsPort=0
dvConfiguration=false
olsConfiguration=false
datafileJarLocation={ORACLE_HOME}/assistants/dbca/templates/
datafileDestination={ORACLE_BASE}/oradata/{DB_UNIQUE_NAME}/
recoveryAreaDestination={ORACLE_BASE}/fast_recovery_area/{DB_UNIQUE_NAME}
storageType=FS
characterSet=AL32UTF8
nationalCharacterSet=AL16UTF16
registerwithDirService=false
listeners=LISTENER
variables=DB_UNIQUE_NAME=CDB1,ORACLE_BASE=/u02/app/oracle,PDB_NAME=,DB_NAME=CDB1,ORACLE_
HOME=/u01/app/oracle/product/12.2.0/dbhome_1,SID=CDB1
initParams=undo_tablespace=UNDOTBS1,processes=300,db_recovery_file_dest_size=10240MB,nls
_language=AMERICAN,pga_aggregate_target=748MB,sga_target=2242MB,dispatchers=(PROTOCOL=TC
P)
(SERVICE=CDB1XDB),db_recovery_file_dest={ORACLE_BASE}/fast_recovery_area/{DB_UNIQUE_NAME
},db_block_size=8192BYTES,diagnostic_dest={ORACLE_BASE},audit_file_dest={ORACLE_BASE}/ad
min/{DB_UNIQUE_NAME}/adump,nls_territory=AMERICA,local_listener=LISTENER_CDB1,log_archiv
e_format=%t_%s_%r.dbf,compatible=12.2.0,control_files=("{ORACLE_BASE}/oradata/{DB_UNIQUE
_NAME}/control01.ctl",
"{ORACLE_BASE}/fast_recovery_area/{DB_UNIQUE_NAME}/control02.ctl"),db_name=CDB1,audit_tr
ail=db,db_domain=compute-
a427312.oraclecloud.internal,remote_login_passwordfile=EXCLUSIVE,open_cursors=300
sampleSchema=true
memoryPercentage=40
databaseType=MULTIPURPOSE
automaticMemoryManagement=false
totalMemory=0
```

Here are the results of issuing this DBCA command. There may be some warnings
about the size of the Fast Recovery Area, but they can be safely ignored.

```
[WARNING] [DBT-06801] Specified Fast Recovery Area size (10,240 MB) is
less than the recommended value.
   CAUSE: Fast Recovery Area size should at least be three times the
database size (3,571 MB).
```

```
   ACTION: Specify Fast Recovery Area Size to be at least three times
the database size.
Copying database files
1% complete
13% complete
25% complete
Creating and starting Oracle instance
26% complete
. . .
Completing Database Creation
. . .
50% complete
Creating Pluggable Databases
55% complete
75% complete
Executing Post Configuration Actions
100% complete
Look at the log file "/u01/app/oracle/cfgtoollogs/dbca/CDB1/CDB1.log"
for further details.
```

Similarly, we'll now create a new CDB named **CDB2** that has no PDBs at all –
essentially, an "empty" Container Database. Again, here's the invocation of DBCA in
silent mode.

```
$> dbca -silent -createDatabase -responseFile
/home/oracle/CDB2_NoPDBs.rsp
```

Below is the response file for CDB2's creation – again, with comments removed for
the sake of brevity.

```
####################################################################
## DBCA Response File:   CDB2_NoPDBs.rsp
## Purpose:              Builds a CDB named CDB2 with no PDBs
## Author:               Jim Czuprynski
## Maintenance Log:
## 1.0  JSC      Initial version
####################################################################
#-----------------------------------------------------------------
# Do not change the following system generated value.
#-----------------------------------------------------------------
responseFileVersion=/oracle/assistants/rspfmt_dbca_response_schema_v12.2.0

#####
# Additional configuration parameters (Comments removed)
#####
gdbName=CDB2.compute-a427312.oraclecloud.internal
sid=CDB2
databaseConfigType=SI
policyManaged=false
createServerPool=false
force=false
createAsContainerDatabase=true
numberOfPDBs=0
useLocalUndoForPDBs=true
templateName=/u01/app/oracle/product/12.2.0/dbhome_1/assistants/dbca/templates/General_P
urpose.dbc
sysPassword=*********
systemPassword=*********
emExpressPort=5501
runCVUChecks=false
omsPort=0
dvConfiguration=false
olsConfiguration=false
datafileJarLocation={ORACLE_HOME}/assistants/dbca/templates/
datafileDestination={ORACLE_BASE}/oradata/{DB_UNIQUE_NAME}/
recoveryAreaDestination={ORACLE_BASE}/fast_recovery_area/{DB_UNIQUE_NAME}
storageType=FS
characterSet=AL32UTF8
nationalCharacterSet=AL16UTF16
registerWithDirService=false
```

```
listeners=LISTENER
variables=DB_UNIQUE_NAME=CDB2,ORACLE_BASE=/u01/app/oracle,PDB_NAME=,DB_NAME=CDB2,ORACLE_
HOME=/u01/app/oracle/product/12.2.0/dbhome_1,SID=CDB2
initParams=undo_tablespace=UNDOTBS1,processes=300,db_recovery_file_dest_size=4096MB,nls_
language=AMERICAN,pga_aggregate_target=748MB,sga_target=2242MB,dispatchers=(PROTOCOL=TCP
)
(SERVICE=CDB2XDB),db_recovery_file_dest={ORACLE_BASE}/fast_recovery_area/{DB_UNIQUE_NAME
},db_block_size=8192BYTES,diagnostic_dest={ORACLE_BASE},audit_file_dest={ORACLE_BASE}/ad
min/{DB_UNIQUE_NAME}/adump,nls_territory=AMERICA,local_listener=LISTENER_CDB2,compatible
=12.2.0,control_files=("{ORACLE_BASE}/oradata/{DB_UNIQUE_NAME}/control01.ctl",
"{ORACLE_BASE}/fast_recovery_area/{DB_UNIQUE_NAME}/control02.ctl"),db_name=CDB2,audit_tr
ail=db,db_domain=compute-
a427312.oraclecloud.internal,remote_login_passwordfile=EXCLUSIVE,open_cursors=300
sampleSchema=false
memoryPercentage=40
databaseType=MULTIPURPOSE
automaticMemoryManagement=false
totalMemory=0
```

Lastly, here is an example of the results of building CDB2 using DBCA in "silent" mode. You may notice some warnings about the size of the Fast Recovery Area, but they can be safely ignored.

```
[WARNING] [DBT-06801] Specified Fast Recovery Area size (4,096 MB) is
less than the recommended value.
    CAUSE: Fast Recovery Area size should at least be three times the
database size (1,936 MB).
. . .
Copying database files
1% complete
2% complete
18% complete
33% complete
Creating and starting Oracle instance
35% complete
40% complete
. . .
55% complete
Completing Database Creation
56% complete
. . .
66% complete
Executing Post Configuration Actions
100% complete
Look at the log file "/u01/app/oracle/cfgtoollogs/dbca/CDB2/CDB2.log"
for further details.
```

Setting Up Security Keystores

Now that both CDBs are rebuilt, you'll set up security keystores for them. This is a crucial step and must not be skipped!

You'll first create appropriate directory structures that will eventually contain each CDB's keystores. Note that each CDB must have its own directory in which to store its TDE encryption keys.

```
$> mkdir /u01/app/oracle/admin/CDB1/tde_wallet
$> mkdir /u01/app/oracle/admin/CDB2/tde_wallet
```

Next, edit the contents of the SQLNET.ORA network configuration file to take advantage of the keystores. It is always a good idea to make a backup of this file in case it should be accidently corrupted.

```
$> cp /u01/app/oracle/product/12.2.0/dbhome_1/network/admin/sqlnet.ora
\
/u01/app/oracle/product/12.2.0/dbhome_1/network/admin/sqlnet.original
```

> *Note:* As experienced Oracle DBAs already know, *SQLNET.ORA* still remains
> as one of the few persnickety network configuration files, so be sure to edit it
> carefully using an editor that is appropriate to the environment you're working
> in. For Linux and UNIX environments, be especially careful when copying
> text from a file edited in a Microsoft Windows environment, and always verify
> the resulting edits with the *vi* editor.

Edit SQLNET.ORA so that the ENCRYPTION_WALLET_LOCATION parameter now allows
each CDB to use a different directory path for its own TDE keystores.

```
$> vi /u01/app/oracle/product/12.2.0/dbhome_1/network/admin/sqlnet.ora

SQLNET.ENCRYPTION_SERVER = required

SQLNET.CRYPTO_CHECKSUM_TYPES_SERVER = (SHA1)

SQLNET.CRYPTO_CHECKSUM_SERVER = required

ENCRYPTION_WALLET_LOCATION = (SOURCE=(METHOD=FILE)
(METHOD_DATA=(DIRECTORY=/u01/app/oracle/admin/$ORACLE_SID/tde_wallet)))

SQLNET.ENCRYPTION_TYPES_SERVER = (AES256, AES192, AES128)

NAMES.DIRECTORY_PATH = (TNSNAMES, EZCONNECT)

SQLNET.WALLET_OVERRIDE = FALSE

SQLNET.EXPIRE_TIME = 10

SSL_VERSION = 1.2

WALLET_LOCATION = (SOURCE=(METHOD=FILE)
(METHOD_DATA=(DIRECTORY=/u01/app/oracle/admin/CDB1/db_wallet)))
```

Let's decode the meaning of the parameters pertinent to TDE:

- **SQLNET.ENCRYPTION_SERVER = required** specifies that advanced security
  is enabled for the database server – essentially, permitting this server to perform
  encryption for its databases.
- **SQLNET.ENCRYPTION_TYPES_SERVER** = (AES256, AES192, AES128)
  specifies the types of encryption algorithms the server can use to manage
  encryption. Note that by default, DBaaS uses the AES128 encryption scheme
  for encrypting tablespaces.
- **ENCRYPTION_WALLET_LOCATION =** ... specifies the exact location for the
  keystore's files. Note that since each CDB needs its own keystore, we include
  the **$ORACLE_SID** environment variable in the path of the specified directory to
  make sure it's unique for each database.

It's time to construct CDB1's keystores and their contents. From within the root
container of CDB1 (CDB$ROOT), we'll create the new keystore with the CREATE
KEYSTORE clause of the ADMINISTER KEY MANAGEMENT command. Note that we're
using the **SYS** user account, but any user account that has key management
privileges granted through the **SYSKM** privilege group will work.

```
$> . oraenv
ORACLE_SID = [oracle] ? CDB1
The Oracle base remains unchanged with value /u01/app/oracle

$> sqlplus / as sysdba
SQL*Plus: Release 12.2.0.1.0 Production on Thu Jun 15 19:07:44 2017
Copyright (c) 1982, 2016, Oracle.  All rights reserved.
Connected to:
Oracle Database 12c Enterprise Edition Release 12.2.0.1.0 - 64bit
Production

SQL> ALTER SESSION SET CONTAINER = cdb$root;
Session altered.

SQL> SHOW CON_NAME
CON_NAME
------------------------------
CDB$ROOT

SQL> ADMINISTER KEY MANAGEMENT
    CREATE KEYSTORE '/u01/app/oracle/admin/CDB1/tde_wallet'
    IDENTIFIED BY "IOU_Geniu5";

Keystore created.
```

If you now check the corresponding directory, you'll notice there is now a new file present named **ewallet.p12**. Each time that a new key is created, a new file will be generated in this directory, but the *original* files are retained for backwards security compatibility.

Still from within **CDB$ROOT**, open the keystore with the **SET KEYSTORE OPEN** clause of the **ADMINISTER KEY MANAGEMENT** command. Note that specifying **CONTAINER = CURRENT** narrows the scope of the opened keystore to just the root container for now:.

```
SQL> ADMINISTER KEY MANAGEMENT
    SET KEYSTORE OPEN FORCE KEYSTORE
    IDENTIFIED BY "IOU_Geniu5"
    CONTAINER = CURRENT;

Keystore altered.
```

Still from within **CDB$ROOT**, create CDB1's TDE master key next with the **SET KEY** clause of the **ADMINISTER KEY MANAGEMENT** command. The **WITH BACKUP** clause actually makes a backup of any prior version of TDE keys in the keystore, because it's necessary to preserve those keys for restoration of an RMAN backup or other encrypted data.

```
SQL> ADMINISTER KEY MANAGEMENT
    SET KEY
    IDENTIFIED BY "IOU_Geniu5"
    WITH BACKUP
    USING "tde_dbaas_bkup";

Keystore altered.
```

To confirm that CDB1's keystore is in the proper state, execute the queries in **ksq.sql**, which show the contents of **V$ENCRYPTION_WALLET** and **V$ENCRYPTION_KEYS**, as well as (eventually) the master keys for the tablespaces of the CDB and its corresponding PDBs.

```
/*
|| Script:  ksq.sql
|| Purpose: Reports various aspects of keystores and TDE encryption
*/


-----
-- What type of encryption is in place?
-----
COL con_id              FORMAT 9999         HEADING "Con|ID"
COL wrl_type            FORMAT A12          HEADING "WRL Type"
COL status              FORMAT A12          HEADING "Status"
COL wallet_type         FORMAT A12          HEADING "Wallet Type"
COL wallet_order        FORMAT A12          HEADING "Wallet Order"
COL fully_backed_up     FORMAT A04          HEADING "Bckd|Up?"
COL wrl_parameter       FORMAT A40          HEADING "WRL Directory"
WRAP
SET LINESIZE 130
SET PAGESIZE 2000
TTITLE "Encryption Key Wallet Information|(from V$ENCRYPTION_WALLET)"
SELECT
     con_id
    ,wrl_type
    ,status
    ,wallet_type
    ,wallet_order
    ,fully_backed_up
    ,wrl_parameter
  FROM v$encryption_wallet;
TTITLE OFF


-----
-- Show encryption keys
-----
COL shortkey            FORMAT A40          HEADING "Keystore Key"
COL shorttag            FORMAT A12          HEADING "Tag"
COL creation_dtm        FORMAT A10          HEADING "Created|On" WRAP
COL activate_dtm        FORMAT A10          HEADING "Activated|At"
WRAP
COL creator             FORMAT A12          HEADING "Creator"
COL creator_id          FORMAT A12          HEADING "Creator|ID"
COL user                FORMAT A12          HEADING "User"
COL user_id             FORMAT A12          HEADING "UserID"
COL key_use             FORMAT A12          HEADING "Key Usage"
COL keystore_type       FORMAT A12          HEADING "Keystore|Type"
COL origin              FORMAT A12          HEADING "Origin"
COL backed_up           FORMAT A04          HEADING "Bckd|Up?"
COL con_id              FORMAT 9999         HEADING "Con|ID"
SET LINESIZE 130
SET PAGESIZE 2000
TTITLE "Encryption Key Values|(from V$ENCRYPTION_KEYS)"
SELECT
     con_id
    ,SUBSTR(key_id,1,40) shortkey
    ,SUBSTR(tag,1,12) shorttag
    ,TO_CHAR(creation_time,'yyyy-mm-dd hh24:mi:ss') creation_dtm
    ,TO_CHAR(activation_time,'yyyy-mm-dd hh24:mi:ss') activate_dtm
    ,key_use
    ,keystore_type
    ,origin
    ,backed_up
  FROM v$encryption_keys;
TTITLE OFF

-----
```

```
-- What are the master keys of all tablespaces in all containers?
-----
COL con_name                FORMAT A10        HEADING "Container"
COL ts_name                 FORMAT A30        HEADING "Tablespace Name"
COL ts#                     FORMAT 99999      HEADING "TSP|#"
COL masterkeyid_base64      FORMAT A30        HEADING "Master Key Value"
BREAK ON name
BREAK ON con_name
SET LINESIZE 80
TTITLE "TDE Master Keys for Tablespaces"
SELECT
    con_name
    ,ts#
    ,name as ts_name
    ,UTL_RAW.CAST_TO_VARCHAR2(
UTL_ENCODE.BASE64_ENCODE('01'||SUBSTR(mkeyid,1,4))) ||
UTL_RAW.CAST_TO_VARCHAR2(UTL_ENCODE.BASE64_ENCODE(SUBSTR(mkeyid,5,LENGT
H(mkeyid)))) masterkeyid_base64
FROM (
    SELECT
        p.name as con_name
        ,t.ts#
        ,t.name
        ,RAWTOHEX(x.mkid) mkeyid
    FROM v$tablespace t, x$kcbtek x, v$pdbs p
    WHERE t.ts# = x.ts#
      AND p.con_id = t.con_id
      AND x.con_id=p.con_id)
ORDER BY con_name, ts#;
TTITLE OFF
```

The output from these queries when run against **CDB1** at the root container level (**CDB$ROOT**) can be seen below.

```
                           Encryption Key Wallet Information
                                (from V$ENCRYPTION_WALLET)

Con                                                Bckd
 ID WRL Type     Status    Wallet Type  Wallet Order Up?    WRL Directory
--- ----------- --------- ------------ ------------ ----- ---------------------------------------
  1 FILE        OPEN      PASSWORD     SINGLE       NO    /u01/app/oracle/admin/CDB1/tde_wallet/


                                Encryption Key Values
                                (from V$ENCRYPTION_KEYS)

Con                                       Created   Activated                Keystore               Bckd
 ID Keystore Key                     Tag  On        At          Key Usage    Type     Origin        Up?
--- -------------------------------- ---- --------- ----------- ------------ -------- ------------- ----
  1 AdXA3y+2d08Bv5wxyJtxkjIAAAAAAAAAAAAAAAAA    2017-09-12 2017-09-12 TDE IN PDB  SOFTWARE KEY LOCAL      NO
                                                02:00:42   02:00:42                          STORE
```

Some interesting things to note:

- The encryption wallet is open for this CDB, and the appropriate directory is being used to locate its keystore.
- The wallet is using password-based methods to open; there are other methods available as well, including an **AUTOLOGIN** feature.
- Only one TDE key has been created so far, and it's stored at the CDB$ROOT level (i.e. CON_ID = 1). Its primary purpose is to provide encryption keys for PDBs.

Building New PDBs for Feature Demonstration

Now that keystores are in place for each CDB, we're ready to proceed with building additional PDBs within CDB1.

First, let's make sure that the PROD_HR PDB is ready to utilize CDB1's keystore. Since CDB1's keystore is not configured for AUTOLOGIN at this point, it's necessary to open the keystore manually for each PDB at this point.

Note: Later in this chapter you'll see how to enable a keystore for AUTOLOGIN, but at this point it's better to leave that feature disabled until all desired PDBs have been deployed.

```
$> . oraenv
ORACLE_SID = [oracle] ? CDB1
The Oracle base remains unchanged with value /u01/app/oracle

$> sqlplus / as sysdba
SQL*Plus: Release 12.2.0.1.0 Production on Thu Jun 15 19:07:44 2017
Copyright (c) 1982, 2016, Oracle.  All rights reserved.
Connected to:
Oracle Database 12c Enterprise Edition Release 12.2.0.1.0 - 64bit
Production

SQL> ADMINISTER KEY MANAGEMENT
     SET KEY
     IDENTIFIED BY "IOU_Genius5"
     WITH BACKUP
     CONTAINER=CURRENT;
*
ERROR at line 1:
ORA-46658: keystore not open in the container
```

This is actually an expected error, because CDB1's keystore is not open at the PDB level. Issue this command to open it for PROD_HR.

```
SQL> ADMINISTER KEY MANAGEMENT
     SET KEYSTORE OPEN FORCE KEYSTORE
     IDENTIFIED BY "IOU_Genius5"
     CONTAINER = CURRENT;

keystore altered.
```

Note the difference in the resulting output from ksq.sql.

```
                            Encryption Key Wallet Information
                               (from V$ENCRYPTION_WALLET)

Con                                          Bckd
 ID WRL Type    Status        Wallet Type Wallet Order Up? WRL Directory
--- --------  ------------  ----------- ------------ ---- ------------------
  3 FILE      OPEN_NO_MAST PASSWORD     SINGLE       UNDE
            ER_KEY                                   FINE
                                                     D


no rows selected

Sun Sep 24                                          page   1
                 TDE Master Keys for Tablespaces
         TSP
```

```
Container        # Tablespace Name              Master Key Value
----------- ------ ---------------------------- ----------------------------
PROD_HR          0 SYSTEM                        AQnUEzjh+k8dv1/7FyG67bU=
                 1 SYSAUX                        AQnUEzjh+k8dv1/7FyG67bU=
                 2 UNDOTBS1                      AQAAAAAAAAAAAAAAAAAAAA=
                 3 TEMP                          AQnUEzjh+k8dv1/7FyG67bU=
```

Next, it's time to set the TDE key value for **PROD_HR** using the **SET KEY** clause of the **ADMINISTER KEY MANAGEMENT** command.

```
SQL> ADMINISTER KEY MANAGEMENT
     SET KEY
     IDENTIFIED BY "IOU_Genius"
     WITH BACKUP
     CONTAINER=CURRENT;

keystore altered.
```

Notice the change in status is now reflected in **V$ENCRYPTION_KEYS**, and the TDE master keys have actually been reset for all of **PROD_HR's** tablespaces.

```
                          Encryption Key Wallet Information
                            (from V$ENCRYPTION_WALLET)

 Con                                                Bckd
  ID  WRL Type    Status      Wallet Type   Wallet Order  Up?  WRL Directory
 ---- --------    ------      -----------   ------------  ----  -------------------------------
   3  FILE        OPEN        PASSWORD      SINGLE        NO

                              Encryption Key Values
                             (from V$ENCRYPTION_KEYS)
 Con
Bckd                                         Created    Activated              Keystore
 ID  Keystore Key                     Tag     On         At      Key Usage     Type       Origin
Up?
---- ---------------------------------------- ---- --------- --------- ----------- ------------ ------------ ----
  3  AYRhwEpWz0+MvS1KLDpVrQoAAAAAAAAAAAAAAAAA      2017-09-24 2017-09-24 TDE IN PDB  SOFTWARE KEY LOCAL       NO
                                                  03:23:40   03:23:40              STORE

                    TDE Master Keys for Tablespaces
                 TSP
Container        # Tablespace Name              Master Key Value
----------- ------ ---------------------------- ----------------------------
PROD_HR          0 SYSTEM                        AYRhwEpWz0+MvS1KLDpVrQo=
                 1 SYSAUX                        AYRhwEpWz0+MvS1KLDpVrQo=
                 2 UNDOTBS1                      AQAAAAAAAAAAAAAAAAAAAA=
                 3 TEMP                          AYRhwEpWz0+MvS1KLDpVrQo=
```

One last maintenance item before we proceed to clone additional PDBs: we'll reset the password for and unlock the **HR** user account on **PROD_HR** so that it won't be necessary to do that each time the PDB is cloned.

```
SQL> ALTER USER hr IDENTIFIED BY hr ACCOUNT UNLOCK;
```

Next, let's create a new PDB named **QA_HR** from the existing **PROD_HR** PDB. Note the use of the **KEYSTORE IDENTIFIED BY** clause to include the rekeying of that PDB's tablespace TDE key.

```
SQL> CREATE PLUGGABLE DATABASE qa_hr
  FROM prod_hr
  FILE_NAME_CONVERT = (
    '/u01/app/oracle/oradata/CDB1/PROD_HR/',
    '/u01/app/oracle/oradata/CDB1/QA_HR/'
  )
  KEYSTORE IDENTIFIED BY "IOU_Genius";

Pluggable database created.

SQL> ALTER PLUGGABLE DATABASE qa_hr OPEN;

Pluggable database altered.
```

Likewise, let's create a new PDB named **DEV_HR** from the existing **PROD_HR** PDB. Again, note the use of the **KEYSTORE IDENTIFIED BY** clause to include the rekeying of that PDB's tablespace TDE key.

```
SQL> CREATE PLUGGABLE DATABASE dev_hr
  FROM prod_hr
  FILE_NAME_CONVERT = (
    '/u01/app/oracle/oradata/CDB1/PROD_HR/',
'/u01/app/oracle/oradata/CDB1/DEV_HR/'
    )
  KEYSTORE IDENTIFIED BY "IOU_Geni u5";
```

Pluggable database created.

```
SQL>ALTER PLUGGABLE DATABASE dev_hr OPEN;
```

Pluggable database altered.

Again, we will create one more PDB named **PROD_AP**. This will be a brand-new PDB that we'll clone from CDB1's **PDB$SEED** PDB, which means it will be empty and ready for us to add our own schemas and corresponding data.

```
SQL> CREATE PLUGGABLE DATABASE prod_ap
  ADMIN USER pdbadmin
  IDENTIFIED BY "IOU_Geni u5"
  FILE_NAME_CONVERT = (
    '/u01/app/oracle/oradata/CDB1/pdbseed/',
    '/u01/app/oracle/oradata/CDB1/PROD_AP/',
    '/u04/app/oracle/oradata/temp/',
    '/u01/app/oracle/oradata/CDB1/PROD_AP/'
    );
```

Pluggable database created.

```
SQL> ALTER PLUGGABLE DATABASE prod_ap OPEN;
```

Pluggable database altered.

To make sure all the TDE security is in place for **PROD_AP**, we'll connect to that PDB and administer its keys as well before creating any new tablespaces or adding new data.

```
SQL> ALTER SESSION SET CONTAINER=PROD_AP;
```

Session altered.

```
SQL> ADMINISTER KEY MANAGEMENT
    SET KEYSTORE OPEN FORCE KEYSTORE
    IDENTIFIED BY "IOU_Geni u5"
    CONTAINER = CURRENT;
```

keystore altered.

```
SQL> ADMINISTER KEY MANAGEMENT
    SET KEY
    FORCE KEYSTORE
    IDENTIFIED BY "IOU_Geni u5"
    WITH BACKUP
    CONTAINER = CURRENT;
```

keystore altered.

Next, it is time to flesh out the **PROD_AP** PDB by:

- Creating new tablespaces to hold data and indexes
- Building a new schema (AP) and related objects
- Populating data into the new AP schema

Note: *Due to its extreme length, the script to populate the AP schema can be found in the Appendices.*

```
/*
|| Script:  APTablespaces.sql
|| Object:  Creates tablespaces for separate storage of data
||          and index segments
*/

DROP TABLESPACE ap_data INCLUDING CONTENTS AND DATAFILES;
CREATE TABLESPACE ap_data
    DATAFILE '/u01/app/oracle/oradata/CDB1/PROD_AP/ap_data.dbf'
    SIZE 100M REUSE
    PERMANENT
    LOGGING
    EXTENT MANAGEMENT LOCAL
    SEGMENT SPACE MANAGEMENT AUTO
;

DROP TABLESPACE ap_idx INCLUDING CONTENTS AND DATAFILES;
CREATE TABLESPACE ap_idx
    DATAFILE '/u01/app/oracle/oradata/CDB1/PROD_AP/ap_idx.dbf'
    SIZE 100M REUSE
    PERMANENT
    LOGGING
    EXTENT MANAGEMENT LOCAL
    SEGMENT SPACE MANAGEMENT AUTO;
```

```
/*
|| Script:  APSetup.sql
|| Object:  Creates sequences, tables, indexes, constraints,
||          and views to illustrate a prototype Accounts Payable
||          (AP) system.
*/

/*
|| Create AP schema
*/

DROP ROLE ap_read_only;
CREATE ROLE ap_read_only;

DROP ROLE ap_secured;
CREATE ROLE ap_secured;

DROP USER ap CASCADE;
CREATE USER ap
    IDENTIFIED BY ap
    DEFAULT TABLESPACE sysaux
    TEMPORARY TABLESPACE temp
    PROFILE DEFAULT
```

```
        QUOTA UNLIMITED ON sysaux
        QUOTA UNLIMITED ON ap_data
        QUOTA UNLIMITED ON ap_idx
;

GRANT CONNECT, RESOURCE TO ap;
GRANT CREATE PROCEDURE TO ap;
GRANT CREATE PUBLIC SYNONYM TO ap;
GRANT CREATE SEQUENCE TO ap;
GRANT CREATE SESSION TO ap;
GRANT CREATE SYNONYM TO ap;
GRANT CREATE TABLE TO ap;
GRANT DROP PUBLIC SYNONYM TO ap;
GRANT EXECUTE ANY PROCEDURE TO ap;

GRANT ap_read_only TO ap;
GRANT ap_read_only TO ap_secured;

DROP TABLE ap.invoice_items CASCADE CONSTRAINTS PURGE;
DROP TABLE ap.invoices CASCADE CONSTRAINTS PURGE;
DROP TABLE ap.vendors CASCADE CONSTRAINTS PURGE;

/*
|| Create AP.VENDORS and related objects
*/

-- Create sequence
DROP SEQUENCE ap.seq_vendor_id;
CREATE SEQUENCE ap.seq_vendor_id
    MINVALUE 1
    MAXVALUE 99999999999999999
    START WITH 100
    INCREMENT BY 1
    NOORDER
    CACHE 20;

-- Create table
CREATE TABLE ap.vendors (
    vendor_id       NUMBER          NOT NULL
    ,active_ind     CHAR(1)         DEFAULT 'Y' NOT NULL
    ,name           VARCHAR2(128)   NOT NULL
    ,address_line_1 VARCHAR2(40)    DEFAULT 'UNDEFINED' NOT NULL
    ,address_line_2 VARCHAR2(40)
    ,address_line_3 VARCHAR2(40)
    ,city           VARCHAR2(40)    NOT NULL
    ,state          CHAR(2)
    ,country        VARCHAR2(30)    NOT NULL
    ,credit_card    VARCHAR2(16)    NOT NULL
    ,credit_limit   NUMBER          NOT NULL
)
    TABLESPACE ap_data;

-- Create indexes and constraints
ALTER TABLE ap.vendors
    ADD CONSTRAINT vendors_pk
    PRIMARY KEY (vendor_id)
    USING INDEX (
        CREATE INDEX ap.vendors_pk_idx
            ON ap.vendors (vendor_id)
            TABLESPACE ap_idx
        );

ALTER TABLE ap.vendors
    ADD CONSTRAINT vendors_active_ck
    CHECK (active_ind IN ('Y','N'));

GRANT SELECT              ON ap.vendors TO ap_read_only;
```

```sql
GRANT INSERT, UPDATE ON ap.vendors TO ap_secured;

/*
|| Create AP.INVOICES and related objects
*/

GRANT REFERENCES ON sh.customers    TO ap;
GRANT SELECT     ON sh.customers    TO ap;
GRANT REFERENCES ON sh.products     TO ap;
GRANT SELECT     ON sh.products     TO ap;

DROP SEQUENCE ap.seq_invoice_id;
CREATE SEQUENCE ap.seq_invoice_id
    MINVALUE 1
    MAXVALUE 99999999999999999
    START WITH 100
    INCREMENT BY 1
    NOORDER
    CACHE 20;

CREATE table ap.invoices (
     invoice_id    NUMBER          NOT NULL
    ,active_ind    CHAR(1)         DEFAULT 'Y' NOT NULL
    ,invoice_type  CHAR(1)         DEFAULT 'C' NOT NULL
    ,vendor_id     NUMBER          NOT NULL
    ,customer_id   NUMBER          NOT NULL
    ,balance_due   NUMBER(15,2)    DEFAULT 0
    ,taxable_amt   NUMBER(15,2)    DEFAULT 0
)
    TABLESPACE ap_data;

ALTER TABLE ap.invoices
    ADD CONSTRAINT invoice_active_ck
    CHECK (active_ind IN ('Y','N'));

ALTER TABLE ap.invoices
    ADD CONSTRAINT invoice_type_ck
    CHECK (invoice_type IN ('C','D'));

ALTER TABLE ap.invoices
    ADD CONSTRAINT invoices_pk
    PRIMARY KEY (invoice_id)
    USING INDEX (
        CREATE INDEX ap.invoices_pk_idx
            ON ap.invoices (invoice_id)
            TABLESPACE ap_idx
        );

ALTER TABLE ap.invoices
    ADD CONSTRAINT invoices_vendor_fk
    FOREIGN KEY (vendor_id)
    REFERENCES ap.vendors (vendor_id);

GRANT SELECT         ON ap.invoices TO ap_read_only;
GRANT INSERT, UPDATE ON ap.invoices TO ap_secured;

/*
|| Create AP.INVOICE_ITEMS and related objects
*/

DROP SEQUENCE ap.seq_invoice_item_id;
CREATE SEQUENCE ap.seq_invoice_item_id
    MINVALUE 1
    MAXVALUE 99999999999999999
    START WITH 100
    INCREMENT BY 1
    NOORDER
```

```
      CACHE 20;

CREATE table ap.invoice_items (
     invoice_id      NUMBER            NOT NULL
    ,line_item_nbr   NUMBER            NOT NULL
    ,active_ind      CHAR(1)           DEFAULT 'Y' NOT NULL
    ,product_id      NUMBER(9)         NOT NULL
    ,qty             NUMBER(9)         NOT NULL
    ,extended_amt    NUMBER(15,2)      DEFAULT 0
    ,taxable_ind     CHAR(1)           DEFAULT 'Y' NOT NULL
)
    TABLESPACE ap_data;

ALTER TABLE ap.invoice_items
    ADD CONSTRAINT invoice_item_active_ck
    CHECK (active_ind IN ('Y','N'));

ALTER TABLE ap.invoice_items
    ADD CONSTRAINT invoice_items_pk
    PRIMARY KEY (invoice_id, line_item_nbr)
    USING INDEX (
        CREATE INDEX ap.invoice_items_pk_idx
            ON ap.invoice_items (invoice_id, line_item_nbr)
            TABLESPACE ap_idx
        );

ALTER TABLE ap.invoice_items
    ADD CONSTRAINT invoice_items_invoice_fk
    FOREIGN KEY (invoice_id)
    REFERENCES ap.invoices (invoice_id);

CREATE INDEX ap.invoice_items_prod_idx
    ON ap.invoice_items (product_id)
    TABLESPACE ap_idx;

GRANT SELECT         ON ap.invoice_items TO ap_read_only;
GRANT INSERT, UPDATE ON ap.invoice_items TO ap_secured;

/*
|| Create reporting view for read-only reporting against
|| AP prototype system
*/

CREATE OR REPLACE VIEW ap.rv_invoice_details (
     vendor_name
    ,vendor_credit_card
    ,vendor_credit_limit
    ,customer_id
    ,invoice_id
    ,invoice_status
    ,line_id
    ,taxable_ind
    ,product_id
    ,qty
    ,extended_amt
)
AS
SELECT
     V.name
    ,V.credit_card
    ,V.credit_limit
    ,I.customer_id
    ,I.invoice_id
    ,I.active_ind
    ,ID.line_item_nbr
    ,ID.taxable_ind
    ,ID.product_id
```

```
      ,ID.qty
      ,ID.extended_amt
   FROM
      ap.vendors V
      ,ap.invoices I
      ,ap.invoice_items ID
 WHERE ID.invoice_id = I.invoice_id
   AND I.vendor_id = V.vendor_id
 WITH READ ONLY
;

GRANT SELECT ON ap.rv_invoice_details TO ap_read_only;

-----
-- Compile package specification and body
------

GRANT EXECUTE ON SYS.DBMS_LOCK TO PUBLIC;

CREATE OR REPLACE PACKAGE ap.pkg_load_generator
/*
|| Package:       AP.PKG_LOAD_GENERATOR
|| Version:       10.2.0.1.0
|| Description:   Generates various different loads on the target
||                database for evalution of various Oracle features.
|| Author:        Jim Czuprynski (G+R)
*/
IS

    PROCEDURE RandomDML(Iteration NUMBER);

END pkg_load_generator;
/

CREATE OR REPLACE PACKAGE BODY AP.pkg_load_generator
/*
|| Package Body:  AP.PKG_LOAD_GENERATOR
|| Version:       10.2.0.1.0
|| Description:   Generates various different loads on the target
||                database for evalution of various Oracle features.
|| Author:        Jim Czuprynski (G+R)
*/
IS

    -----
    -- Local VARRAY variables for storage and retrieval of random
    -- values for Customer, Product, and Vendor IDs
    -----

    TYPE va_customer_ids
        IS VARRAY(20) OF PLS_INTEGER;
    TYPE va_list_prices
        IS VARRAY(05) OF NUMBER;
    TYPE va_product_ids
        IS VARRAY(05) OF PLS_INTEGER;
    TYPE va_vendor_ids
        IS VARRAY(10) OF PLS_INTEGER;

    custids     va_customer_ids;
    prices      va_list_prices;
    prodids     va_product_ids;
    vendids     va_vendor_ids;

    /*
    || Private Functions and Procedures
    */

    FUNCTION next_id (
        aOwner      IN VARCHAR2
```

```
        ,aTableName IN VARCHAR2
        ,aKeyID     IN VARCHAR2
        )
    RETURN NUMBER
   /*
   || Function:     Randomizer
   || Purpose:      Retrieves the next available ID for the supplied
combination
   ||               of Table Owner, Table Name, and Key ID using the
appropriate
   ||               sequence object
   || Scope:        Private
   || Arguments:    aOwner       VARCHAR2    Table Owner
   ||               aTableName   VARCHAR2    Table Name
   ||               aKeyID       VARCHAR2    Column Name
   ||
   || Returns:      NewValue     NUMBER
   */
   IS
       NewValue    NUMBER := 0;
   BEGIN
       CASE UPPER(aOwner)
           WHEN 'AP' THEN
               CASE UPPER(aTableName)
                   WHEN 'INVOICES' THEN
                       CASE UPPER(aKeyID)
                           WHEN 'INVOICE_ID' THEN
                               SELECT ap.seq_invoice_id.NEXTVAL
                                   INTO NewValue
                                   FROM DUAL;
                           ELSE
                               NewValue := 0;
                       END CASE;
                   WHEN 'INVOICE_ITEMS' THEN
                       CASE UPPER(aKeyID)
                           WHEN 'LINE_ITEM_NBR' THEN
                               SELECT ap.seq_invoice_item_id.NEXTVAL
                                   INTO NewValue
                                   FROM DUAL;
                           ELSE
                               NewValue := 0;
                       END CASE;
                   WHEN 'VENDORS' THEN
                       CASE UPPER(aKeyID)
                           WHEN 'VENDOR_ID' THEN
                               SELECT ap.seq_vendor_id.NEXTVAL
                                   INTO NewValue
                                   FROM DUAL;
                           ELSE
                               NewValue := 0;
                       END CASE;
                   ELSE
                       NewValue := 0;
               END CASE;
           ELSE
               NewValue := 0;
       END CASE;

       RETURN NewValue;

   EXCEPTION
       WHEN NO_DATA_FOUND THEN
           RETURN -1;
       WHEN OTHERS THEN
           RETURN -2;

   END next_id;
```

```
FUNCTION Randomizer (
      aColumnID VARCHAR2
      ,Iteration NUMBER
)
  RETURN NUMBER
/*
|| Function:     Randomizer
|| Purpose:      Returns a randomized value from one of several
||                dimension tables
|| Scope:        Private
|| Arguments:    aColumnID    VARCHAR2   Column Identifier
||               Iteration    NUMBER     Iteration Number
||
|| Returns:      RandomValue  NUMBER
*/
IS
    RandomValue NUMBER := 0;
BEGIN
    CASE aColumnID
        -- Locate a randomized Customer ID
            WHEN 'cust_id' THEN
                RandomValue := custids((MOD(Iteration, 20)) + 1);
        -- Locate a randomized List Price
            WHEN 'list_price' THEN
                RandomValue := ROUND(prices((MOD(Iteration,   5) +
1)),2);
        -- Locate a randomized Product ID
            WHEN 'product_id' THEN
                RandomValue := prodids((MOD(Iteration,  5) + 1));
        -- Locate a randomized Vendor ID
            WHEN 'vendor_id' THEN
                RandomValue := vendids((MOD(Iteration, 10) + 1));
        ELSE
            RandomValue := 0;
    END CASE;

    RETURN RandomValue;

EXCEPTION
    WHEN OTHERS THEN
        RETURN 0;
END Randomizer;

FUNCTION Randomizer (seed NUMBER)
RETURN NUMBER
/*
|| Function:     Randomizer
|| Purpose:      Returns a randomized number from 1 to 100
||                based on the seed value supplied
|| Scope:        Private
|| Arguments:    seed - Input from calling routine
|| Returns:      Iteration - Randomized number
*/
IS
    Iteration NUMBER := 0;
BEGIN
    SYS.DBMS_RANDOM.SEED(seed);
    Iteration := ROUND(SYS.DBMS_RANDOM.VALUE(1,100));
    SYS.DBMS_RANDOM.TERMINATE;
    RETURN Iteration;
EXCEPTION
    WHEN OTHERS THEN
        RETURN 0;
END Randomizer;

/*
```

```
    || Public Functions and Procedures
  */

  PROCEDURE RandomDML (Iteration NUMBER)
  /*
    || Procedure:    RandomDML
    || Purpose:      Loads a random number of Invoices and Invoice
Details
    ||               into tables AP.INVOICES and AP.INVOICE_ITEMS.
    || Scope:        Public
    || Arguments:    Iteration - Maximum number of Invoices to create
  */
  IS
     InvLoopEnd    NUMBER(9) := 0;
     ItmLoopEnd    NUMBER(9) := 0;
     nInvoiceID    NUMBER(9);
     nVendorID     NUMBER(9);
     nCustID       NUMBER(9);
     nItemID       NUMBER(9);
     nProdID       NUMBER(9);
     nQty          NUMBER(9);
     nListPrice    NUMBER(15,2);
     nExtdAmt      NUMBER(15,2);
     nBalance      NUMBER(15,2);
     aTxblInd      CHAR(1);
     nTxblAmt      NUMBER(15,2);

  BEGIN
     -----
     -- 1.) Calculate number of Invoices to create
      -- 2.) Calculate randomized value for Customer ID
      -- 3.) Calculate next value for Invoice ID
     -----
     InvLoopEnd := Iteration;
     nCustID := Randomizer('cust_id', Iteration);

     /*
     || Invoices generation
     */
     FOR idx1 IN 1..InvLoopEnd
        LOOP
           DBMS_APPLICATION_INFO.SET_MODULE(
                 module_name => 'DMLGenerator'
                ,action_name => 'BuildInvoices'
           );
         nInvoiceID := Next_ID('AP','INVOICES','INVOICE_ID');
           nVendorID := Randomizer('vendor_id', idx1);
           INSERT INTO ap.invoices (
                 invoice_id
                ,active_ind
                ,invoice_type
                ,vendor_id
                ,customer_id
                ,balance_due
                ,taxable_amt
           )
           VALUES(
                 nInvoiceID
                ,'Y'
                ,'C'
                ,nVendorID
                ,nCustID
                ,0
                ,0
           );
           /*
```

```
               || Invoice Line Items generation
             */
                 ItmLoopEnd := Randomizer(InvLoopEnd);
                 nBalance := 0;
                 nTxblAmt := 0;

                 FOR idx2 IN 1..ItmLoopEnd
                    LOOP
                       -- Determine randomized value of number of
invoice items
                       DBMS_APPLICATION_INFO.SET_MODULE(
                           module_name => 'DMLGenerator'
                          ,action_name => 'BuildInvoiceDetail'
                       );

                       -- Calculate next value for Invoice Line Item
Number
                       nItemID :=
Next_ID('AP','INVOICE_ITEMS','LINE_ITEM_NBR');

                       -- Determine randomized value for Product ID and
Quantity
                       nProdID     := Randomizer('product_id', idx2);
                       nListPrice  := Randomizer('list_price', idx2);
                       nQty        := Randomizer(idx2);
                       nExtdAmt    := (nQty * nListPrice);

                       IF MOD(nqty,7) = 0 THEN
                           aTxblInd := 'N';
                       ELSE
                           aTxblInd := 'Y';
                       END IF;

                       -- Add new Invoice Items row
                       INSERT INTO ap.invoice_items (
                               invoice_id
                              ,line_item_nbr
                              ,active_ind
                              ,product_id
                              ,qty
                              ,extended_amt
                              ,taxable_ind
                           )
                       VALUES(
                               nInvoiceID
                              ,nItemID
                              ,'Y'
                              ,nProdID
                              ,nQty
                              ,nExtdAmt
                              ,aTxblInd
                           );

                       nBalance := nBalance + nExtdAmt;
                       IF aTxblInd = 'Y' THEN
                           nTxblAmt := nTxblAmt + nExtdAmt;
                       ELSE
                           nTxblAmt := nTxblAmt;
                       END IF;

                 END LOOP;

                 -- Finally, update Invoice total amounts from
accumulators
                 UPDATE ap.invoices
                    SET
                        balance_due = nBalance
```

```
                        ,taxable_amt = nTxblAmt
                  WHERE invoice_id = nInvoiceID;

         END LOOP;

         /*
         || Finally, pause to allow work to complete
         */
         DBMS_APPLICATION_INFO.SET_MODULE(
           module_name => 'DMLGenerator'
           ,action_name => 'PauseToReflect'
         );
         SYS.DBMS_LOCK.SLEEP(5);

    EXCEPTION
        WHEN OTHERS THEN
            DBMS_OUTPUT.PUT_LINE('Fatal error during processing of
Invoice #' || nInvoiceID);
            ROLLBACK;
    END RandomDML;

BEGIN
    -- Initialize VARRAY values for Randomizer function
    custids :=
            va_customer_ids( 1680,  1743,  1838,   3087,   3453,
                      3592,  3643,  4090,   4974,   6265,
                             6395,  7178,  7571,   7868,   7902,
                             7994,  8563,  8937, 10747, 11407);
    prices  := va_list_prices (1.85, 9.50, 4.83, 55.73, 89.74);
    prodids := va_product_ids (18,    19,    48,   114,   119);
    vendids := va_vendor_ids (105,   135,   163,   185,   193,
                       210,   111,   233,   263,   154);

END pkg_load_generator;
/

GRANT EXECUTE ON ap.pkg_load_generator TO PUBLIC;


/*
|| Script:  Create_ADO_Tablespaces.sql
|| Purpose: Builds tablespaces for "cold" ADO policies
||          on Tier 1 storage
*/

DROP TABLESPACE ado_cold_data INCLUDING CONTENTS AND DATAFILES;
CREATE TABLESPACE ado_cold_data
    DATAFILE '/u01/app/oracle/oradata/CDB1/PROD_AP/ado_cold_data.dbf'
    SIZE 100M
    AUTOEXTEND ON
    MAXSIZE UNLIMITED
    PERMANENT
    LOGGING
    EXTENT MANAGEMENT LOCAL
    SEGMENT SPACE MANAGEMENT AUTO;

DROP TABLESPACE ado_cold_idx INCLUDING CONTENTS AND DATAFILES;
CREATE TABLESPACE ado_cold_idx
    DATAFILE '/u01/app/oracle/oradata/CDB1/PROD_AP/ado_cold_idx.dbf'
    SIZE 100M
    AUTOEXTEND ON
    MAXSIZE UNLIMITED
    PERMANENT
    LOGGING
    EXTENT MANAGEMENT LOCAL
    SEGMENT SPACE MANAGEMENT AUTO
```

```
;
ALTER USER ap QUOTA UNLIMITED on ado_cold_data;
ALTER USER ap QUOTA UNLIMITED on ado_cold_idx;
```

Confirming Successful PDB Setup

Before moving on to actual experiments and explorations, we'll quickly peruse the
progress we've made so far from a PDB perspective. Let's connect to our two
container databases via SQLPlus and confirm the state of all PDBs using the utility
script pdbstate.sql.

```
/*
|| Script:  pdbstate.sql
|| Purpose: Checks current state of PDBs
*/

SET PAGESIZE 5000

SET LINESIZE 40
TTITLE "PDB Status|(from V$PDBS)"
COL name          FORMAT A08      HEADING "PDB|Name"
COL open_mode     FORMAT A12      HEADING "Open|Mode"
SELECT name, open_mode
  FROM v$pdbs
 ORDER BY 1;

SET LINESIZE 60
TTITLE "PDB Status|(from CDB_PDBS)"
COL pdb_name          FORMAT A08        HEADING "PDB|Name"
COL status            FORMAT A12        HEADING "Status"
COL logging           FORMAT A12        HEADING "Logging?"
COL is_proxy_pdb      FORMAT A05        HEADING "Proxy|PDB?"
COL refresh_mode      FORMAT A08        HEADING "Refresh|Mode"
COL refresh_interval  FORMAT 99999      HEADING "Rfrsh|Intvl"
SELECT
      pdb_name
     ,status
     ,logging
     ,is_proxy_pdb
     ,refresh_mode
     ,refresh_interval
  FROM cdb_pdbs
 ORDER BY 1,2;

TTITLE OFF
```

Here's an example of executing that script against the CDB1 database. You should
see that there are **four** PDBs – PROD_AP, PROD_HR, QA_HR, and DEV_AP – plus the
PDB$SEED "seed" PDB in CDB1.

```
$> . oraenv
ORACLE_SID = [oracle] ? CDB1
The Oracle base remains unchanged with value /u01/app/oracle

$> sqlplus / as sysdba
SQL*Plus: Release 12.2.0.1.0 Production on Thu Jun 15 19:07:44 2017
Copyright (c) 1982, 2016, Oracle.  All rights reserved.
Connected to:
Oracle Database 12c Enterprise Edition Release 12.2.0.1.0 - 64bit
Production
```

```
SQL@CDB1> @pdbstate.sql

                PDB Status
               (from V$PDBS)

PDB        Open
Name       Mode
--------   ------------
DEV_AP     READ WRITE
PDB$SEED   READ ONLY
PROD_AP    READ WRITE
PROD_HR    READ WRITE
QA_HR      READ WRITE
                             PDB Status
                           (from CDB_PDBS)

PDB                                      Proxy  Refresh   Rfrsh
Name       Status        Logging?        PDB?   Mode      Intvl
--------   ------------  ------------    -----  --------  ------
DEV_AP     NORMAL        LOGGING         NO     NONE
PDB$SEED   NORMAL        LOGGING         NO     NONE
PROD_AP    NORMAL        LOGGING         NO     NONE
PROD_HR    NORMAL        LOGGING         NO     NONE
QA_HR      NORMAL        LOGGING         NO     NONE
```

Only the **PDB$SEED** "seed" PDB present in CDB2:

```
$> . oraenv
ORACLE_SID = [oracle] ? CDB2
The Oracle base remains unchanged with value /u01/app/oracle

$> sqlplus / as sysdba
SQL*Plus: Release 12.2.0.1.0 Production on Thu Jun 15 19:07:44 2017
Copyright (c) 1982, 2016, Oracle.  All rights reserved.
Connected to:
Oracle Database 12c Enterprise Edition Release 12.2.0.1.0 - 64bit
Production

SQL@CDB2> @pdbstate.sql

                PDB Status
               (from V$PDBS)

PDB        Open
Name       Mode
--------   ------------
PDB$SEED   READ ONLY

                             PDB Status
                           (from CDB_PDBS)

PDB                                      Proxy  Refresh   Rfrsh
Name       Status        Logging?        PDB?   Mode      Intvl
--------   ------------  ------------    -----  --------  ------
PDB$SEED   NORMAL        LOGGING         NO     NONE
```

Completing Network Connectivity for PDBs

Now, perform one last step to allow connectivity to your new CDBs and PDBs from any client machines: add or replace the following lines in `TNSNAMES.ORA,` editing them appropriately to reflect the host names and service names of each CDB and PDB.

```
LISTENER_CDB1 =
  (ADDRESS =
    (PROTOCOL = TCP)
    (HOST = PDBME.compute-a427312.oraclecloud.internal)
    (PORT = 1521)
  )

LISTENER_CDB2 =
  (ADDRESS =
    (PROTOCOL = TCP)
    (HOST = PDBME.compute-a427312.oraclecloud.internal)
    (PORT = 1521)
  )

CDB1 =
  (DESCRIPTION =
    (ADDRESS =
        (PROTOCOL = TCP)
        (HOST = PDBME.compute-a427312.oraclecloud.internal)
        (PORT = 1521))
    (CONNECT_DATA =
      (SERVER = DEDICATED)
      (SERVICE_NAME = CDB1.compute-a427312.oraclecloud.internal)
    )
  )

CDB2 =
  (DESCRIPTION =
    (ADDRESS =
        (PROTOCOL = TCP)
        (HOST = PDBME.compute-a427312.oraclecloud.internal)
        (PORT = 1521))
    (CONNECT_DATA =
      (SERVER = DEDICATED)
      (SERVICE_NAME = CDB2.compute-a427312.oraclecloud.internal)
    )
  )

PROD_AP =
  (DESCRIPTION =
    (ADDRESS =
        (PROTOCOL = TCP)
        (HOST = PDBME.compute-a427312.oraclecloud.internal)
        (PORT = 1521))
    (CONNECT_DATA =
      (SERVER = DEDICATED)
      (SERVICE_NAME = prod_ap.compute-a427312.oraclecloud.internal)
    )
  )

PROD_HR =
  (DESCRIPTION =
    (ADDRESS =
        (PROTOCOL = TCP)
        (HOST = PDBME.compute-a427312.oraclecloud.internal)
        (PORT = 1521))
    (CONNECT_DATA =
      (SERVER = DEDICATED)
      (SERVICE_NAME = prod_hr.compute-a427312.oraclecloud.internal)
    )
```

```
     )
QA_HR =
  (DESCRIPTION =
    (ADDRESS =
        (PROTOCOL = TCP)
        (HOST = PDBME.compute-a427312.oraclecloud.internal)
        (PORT = 1521))
    (CONNECT_DATA =
      (SERVER = DEDICATED)
      (SERVICE_NAME = qa_hr.compute-a427312.oraclecloud.internal)
    )
  )

DEV_HR =
  (DESCRIPTION =
    (ADDRESS =
        (PROTOCOL = TCP)
        (HOST = PDBME.compute-a427312.oraclecloud.internal)
        (PORT = 1521))
    (CONNECT_DATA =
      (SERVER = DEDICATED)
      (SERVICE_NAME = dev_hr.compute-a427312.oraclecloud.internal)
    )
  )
```

Creating Security Keystore for CDB2

You are now almost done! Let's execute this code for the CDB2 container database
to create and initialize its keystore. Since there are no PDBs resident within this CDB
yet, that's all that's required for now.

```
$> . oraenv
ORACLE_SID = [oracle] ? CDB2
The Oracle base remains unchanged with value /u01/app/oracle

$> sqlplus / as sysdba
SQL*Plus: Release 12.2.0.1.0 Production on Thu Jun 15 19:07:44 2017
Copyright (c) 1982, 2016, Oracle.  All rights reserved.
Connected to:
Oracle Database 12c Enterprise Edition Release 12.2.0.1.0 - 64bit
Production

SQL> ALTER SESSION SET CONTAINER = cdb$root;

Session altered.

-- Create Keystore
SQL> ADMINISTER KEY MANAGEMENT
    CREATE KEYSTORE '/u01/app/oracle/admin/CDB2/tde_wallet'
    IDENTIFIED BY "IOU_Geniu5";

Keystore created.

-- Open Keystore
SQL> ADMINISTER KEY MANAGEMENT
    SET KEYSTORE OPEN FORCE KEYSTORE
    IDENTIFIED BY "IOU_Geniu5"
    CONTAINER = ALL;

Keystore altered.
```

```
-- Set the CDB's TDE key in the Keystore
SQL> ADMINISTER KEY MANAGEMENT
    SET KEY
    IDENTIFIED BY "IOU_Geniu5"
    WITH BACKUP
    USING "tde_dbaas_bkup";

Keystore altered.
```

Enabling a Keystore for AUTOLOGIN

Now that all keystores have been created at the CDB level and TDE security has been applied to all user tablespaces at the PDB level; we can choose a simpler method to enable opening and closing the security key wallets, at both the CDB and PDB level by enabling AUTOLOGIN mode for the keystores.

```
SQL> ALTER SESSION SET CONTAINER = cdb$root;

Session altered.

SQL> ADMINISTER KEY MANAGEMENT
    CREATE AUTO_LOGIN KEYSTORE
    FROM KEYSTORE '/u01/app/oracle/admin/CDB1/tde_wallet'
    IDENTIFIED BY "IOU_Geniu5";

Keystore altered.
```

If you query the contents of the directory that's storing the keystore files, you'll now notice that a new file, **cwallet.sso**, exists – and that's where the keystore's AUTOLOGIN credentials are retained. Interestingly, however, querying V$ENCRYPTION_WALLET immediately after performing this step reveals that the wallet type is still PASSWORD.

```
Encryption Key Wallet Information
 (from V$ENCRYPTION_WALLET)

 Con
  ID WRL Type    Status       Wallet Type  Wallet Order
----- -----------  -----------  -----------  ------------
   1 FILE         OPEN         PASSWORD     SINGLE
```

Unfortunately, the keystore won't be assigned its new AUTOLOGIN status until the database instance has been restarted.

```
SQL> ALTER SESSION SET CONTAINER = cdb$root;

Session altered.

SQL> shutdown immediate;

Database closed.
Database dismounted.
ORACLE instance shut down.

SQL>startup;

ORACLE instance started.

Total System Global Area 2365587456 bytes
Fixed Size                  8795472 bytes
```

```
Variable Size                654314160 bytes
Database Buffers            1694498816 bytes
Redo Buffers                  7979008 bytes

Database mounted.
Database opened.
```

Only now **V$ENCRYPTION_WALLET** does reflect the new status of **AUTOLOGIN**:

```
Encryption Key Wallet Information
 (from V$ENCRYPTION_WALLET)

 Con
  ID WRL Type      Status         Wallet Type  Wallet Order
 ----- ------------ ------------  -----------  ------------
   1 FILE          OPEN           AUTOLOGIN    SINGLE
```

When opening this CDB's **CDB$ROOT** container or any PDB within that container, you won't need to open the keystore manually, via the **ADMINISTER KEY MANAGEMENT SET KEYSTORE OPEN** command.

Disabling and Re-Enabling AUTOLOGIN Mode

Now, a warning: Enabling **AUTOLOGIN** mode for keystores may appear to be desirable, but be aware of a rather intriguing issue – we'd hesitate to call it a bug, and it's too annoying to be called a feature. With **AUTOLOGIN** keystores, when it's time to create a new tablespace at the PDB level, it may be necessary to deactivate and then reactivate **AUTOLOGIN** mode through the following rather tedious steps.

1.) Remove the **cwallet.sso** file from the appropriate directory. This essentially drops the **AUTOLOGIN** capability, because that's where Oracle stores the security key containing the login for the wallet file.

2.) Close the wallet at the CDB level.

```
SQL> ADMINISTER KEY MANAGEMENT
      SET KEYSTORE CLOSE;

Keystore altered.
```

3.) Rekey the CDB. Unfortunately, this is apparently the only way to make this work, at least in this most recent release of Oracle Database 12.2.0.1.

```
SQL> ALTER SESSION SET CONTAINER = cdb$root;

Session altered.

SQL> ADMINISTER KEY MANAGEMENT
      SET KEYSTORE OPEN
      IDENTIFIED BY "IOU_Geniu5"
      CONTAINER=CURRENT;

Keystore altered.

SQL> ADMINISTER KEY MANAGEMENT
      SET KEY
      IDENTIFIED BY "IOU_Geniu5"
      WITH BACKUP
      CONTAINER=CURRENT;
```

Keystore altered.

```
SQL> ADMINISTER KEY MANAGEMENT
     CREATE AUTO_LOGIN KEYSTORE
     FROM KEYSTORE '/u01/app/oracle/admin/CDB1/tde_wallet'
     IDENTIFIED BY "IOU_Geni u5";
```

Keystore altered.

4.) Rekey each desired PDB using the same steps above, but not before issuing the **ALTER SESSION SET CONTAINER** = <*pdb_name*>; for each desired PDB.

5.) Finally, recreate the **AUTOLOGIN** keystore at the CDB level using the same command we originally used.

```
SQL> ADMINISTER KEY MANAGEMENT
     CREATE AUTO_LOGIN KEYSTORE
     FROM KEYSTORE '/u01/app/oracle/admin/CDB1/tde_wallet'
     IDENTIFIED BY "IOU_Geni u5";
```

Keystore altered.

5. Leveraging Oracle Public Cloud DBaaS REST API

So far we've only demonstrated the use of the OPC DBaaS web-based interface to control and monitor the status of service instances. There is another, much simpler, way to handle this without any graphic user interface at all: via scripted calls to the OPC DBaaS *Representational State Transfer* (REST) API.

The REST API is well documented, simple to learn and implement via almost any scripting language, and provides an extremely thin layer of calls between a controlling environment and OPC DBaaS service instances. Documentation for the OPC DBaaS API is available at https://docs.oracle.com/en/cloud/paas/database-dbaas-cloud/csdbr/index.html.

To demonstrate how easy it is to leverage the REST API, here are some simple examples for managing service instances using the popular CURL scripting language. We strongly recommend cracking open the documentation while experimenting with these scripts, especially if this is your first time leveraging this powerful API.

Viewing Instance Status

Here's an example of a CURL script that invokes the GET REST API method to display the status of all instances for the DBaaS domain named a427312.

```
curl --include --request GET \
--user 'jczupryn@zdc.com:IOU_Geniu5' \
--header "X-ID-TENANT-NAME:a427312" \
https://dbaas.oraclecloud.com/paas/service/dbcs/api/v1.1/instances/a427312
```

To see just a single instance's status, it's only necessary to tack on the instance to the domain.

```
curl --include --request GET \
--user 'jczupryn@zdc.com:IOU_Geniu5' \
--header "X-ID-TENANT-NAME:a427312" \
https://dbaas.oraclecloud.com/paas/service/dbcs/api/v1.1/instances/a427312/PDBME
```

For reviewing information about all of the compute nodes of an instance, tack on the servers keyword.

```
curl --include --request GET \
--user 'jczupryn@zdc.com:IOU_Geniu5' \
--header "X-ID-TENANT-NAME:a427312" \
https://dbaas.oraclecloud.com/paas/service/dbcs/api/v1.1/instances/a427312/PDBME/servers
```

Creating an Instance

To create a new service instance, leverage the POST method to send over a series of specifications formatted within a JSON script.

```
curl --include --request POST \
--user 'jczupryn@zdc.com:IOU_Geniu5' \
--header "X-ID-TENANT-NAME:a427312" \
--header "Content-Type:application/json" \
--data @CreateInstance.json \
https://dbaas.oraclecloud.com/paas/service/dbcs/api/v1.1/instances/a427
312
```

The `CreateInstance` JSON script that actually builds the requested instance in that domain can be seen below.

```
{
    "serviceName": "PDBME",
    "description": "DBAAS 12.2 PDB Instance",
    "shape": "oc3",
    "vmPublicKeyText": "ssh-rsa AAAAB3***[redacted]***5Ha8wYN",
    "subscriptionType": "HOURLY",
    "level": "PAAS",
    "version": "12.2.0.1",
    "edition": "EE",
    "parameters": [
        {
            "type": "db",
            "usableStorage": "25",
            "adminPassword": "R3D5cT#d",
            "sid": "CDB1",
            "pdbName": "PDB1",
            "timezone": "US/Central",
            "ncharset": "AL16UTF16",
            "charset": "AL32UTF8",
            "isRac": "no",
            "failoverDatabase": "no",
            "disasterRecovery": "no",
            "goldenGate": "no",
            "backupDestination": "NONE",
            "additionalParams": {
                "db_demo": "yes"
            }
        }
    ]
}
```

Controlling Domain Instances

To *restart* an existing instance, leverage the POST method and pass over the Restart option of the lifecycleState command.

```
curl --include --request POST \
--user 'jczupryn@zdc.com:IOU_Geniu5' \
--header "X-ID-TENANT-NAME:a427312" \
--header "Content-Type:application/json" \
--data '{ "lifecycleState" : "Restart" }' \
https://dbaas.oraclecloud.com/paas/service/dbcs/api/v1.1/instances/a427
312/PDBME
```

To stop a running instance, the Stop option of the lifecycleState command is used. Note that the lifecycleTimeout parameter controls how long to wait (in minutes) before the request self-terminates. The default time is 60 minutes.

```
curl --include --request POST \
--user 'jczupryn@zdc.com:IOU_Geniu5' \
--header "X-ID-TENANT-NAME:a427312" \
--header "Content-Type:application/json" \
--data '{ "lifecycleState" : "Stop", "lifecycleTimeout" : "5" }' \
https://dbaas.oraclecloud.com/paas/service/dbcs/api/v1.1/instances/a427
312/PDBME
```

The below CURL script *starts* a stopped instance.

```
curl --include --request POST \
--user 'jczupryn@zdc.com:IOU_Geniu5' \
--header "X-ID-TENANT-NAME:a427312" \
--header "Content-Type:application/json" \
--data '{ "lifecycleState" : "Start" }' \
https://dbaas.oraclecloud.com/paas/service/dbcs/api/v1.1/instances/a427
312/PDBME
```

Finally, to *remove* an instance from a particular domain, the DELETE method is used.

```
curl --include --request DELETE \
--user 'jczupryn@zdc.com:IOU_Geniu5' \
--header "X-ID-TENANT-NAME:a427312" \
https://dbaas.oraclecloud.com/paas/service/dbcs/api/v1.1/instances/a427
312/PDBME
```

Note: These CURL script examples barely scratch the surface of what the REST API can do. To view the myriad of Oracle REST APIs features for IaaS, PaaS, and SaaS, consult the Oracle API Cloud Service website (https://apicatalog.oraclecloud.com/ui/). There are excellent, easy-to-follow examples of each API call, and even a "try-it" endpoint for experimentation and skill-building.

---

6. PDB Migration and Refreshes

Oracle Database 12cR1 (12.1.0.1) was the first release to introduce the concept of multitenant databases. The initial multitenant features were quite primitive, but with the next release (12.1.0.2) significant improvements were made. However, it wasn't until the 12cR2 release (12.2.0.1) that multitenancy really reached sufficient maturity, especially in terms of PDB availability.

This chapter will explore three of the newest features of Oracle Database 12.2.0.1 multitenancy that make it extremely capable and pliable for an OPC DBaaS environment:

- **Hot Migration**: the ability to move an existing PDB from one CDB to another even while transactions continue against the PDB in its original location.

- **Refreshable PDBs**: the capability to apply transactional changes made within a "master" PDB against a read-only copy of that master PDB's data, either on an on-demand manual basis, or on a regular schedule.

- **Proxy PDBs**: the ability to create a *proxy* – essentially, a *reference pointer* - to an existing PDB, but stll perform all DDL and DML as if we were performing the transactions natively against the referenced PDB.

PDB "Hot" Migration

Use Case: The QA_HR PDB needs to be migrated from container database CDB1 to CDB2 so that our QA team can assess the performance and viability independently of other PDBs. However, since the QA team is also performing DML testing against QA_HR, we need to migrate this PDB without shutting it down and with only limited interruption to service. Therefore, we'll employ 12.2's new "hot" PDB migration feature to migrate this PDB.

First create a common user named C##LINKUP, we'll use this when creating public database links between CDB1 and CDB2 using the commands in script `Create_C##_Linkup.sql`.

```
/*
|| Script:  Create_C##LINKUP.sql
|| Purpose: Creates common user on CDB1 and CDB2 and all current PDBs
for
||          purposes of database links
*/

DROP USER c##linkup CASCADE;
CREATE USER c##linkup
    IDENTIFIED BY oracle_4U
    CONTAINER=ALL
;

GRANT CREATE SESSION TO c##linkup CONTAINER=ALL;
GRANT SYSOPER TO c##linkup CONTAINER=ALL;
GRANT CREATE PLUGGABLE DATABASE TO c##linkup CONTAINER=ALL;

-- Not needed for this exercise
-- Added by CKIM for Proxy DB Exercise
GRANT SELECT ANY DICTIONARY TO c##linkup CONTAINER=ALL;
```

Via SQL*Plus, execute the same script on **both** CDB1 and CDB2.
From **CDB1**:

```
SQL@CDB1> @Create_C##LINKUP.sql

DROP USER c##linkup CASCADE
ERROR at line 1:
ORA-01918: user 'C##LINKUP' does not exist

User created.

Grant succeeded.

Grant succeeded.

Grant succeeded.

Grant succeeded.
```

Now, from **CDB2**:

```
SQL@CDB2> @Create_C##LINKUP.sql
DROP USER c##linkup CASCADE
ERROR at line 1:
ORA-01918: user 'C##LINKUP' does not exist
```

```
User created.

Grant succeeded.

Grant succeeded.

Grant succeeded.

Grant succeeded.
```

Note that the `C##LINKUP` user account will also be granted sufficient privileges to create a pluggable database.

Next, let's create public database links between CDB1 and CDB2 using the new `C##LINKUP` common user. We'll use the commands in script `Create_CDB1_Link.sql`:

```
/*
|| Script:  Create_CDB1_Link.sql
|| Purpose: Create PUBLIC database link from CDB1 to CDB2
*/

-- RUN THIS FROM CDB1!!!

DROP PUBLIC DATABASE LINK pdbback;
CREATE PUBLIC DATABASE LINK pdbback
    CONNECT TO c##linkup IDENTIFIED BY oracle_4U
    USING 'CDB2';

SELECT name, open_mode from v$database@pdbback;
```

From CDB1, execute:

```
SQL@CDB1> @Create_CDB1_Link.sql
DROP PUBLIC DATABASE LINK pdbback
                         *
ERROR at line 1:
ORA-02024: database link not found

Database link created.

PDB       Open
Name      Mode
--------  ------------
CDB2      READ WRITE
```

Then from CDB2, execute script `Create_CDB2_Link.sql`, shown below:

```
/*
|| Script:  Create_CDB2_Link.sql
|| Purpose: Create PUBLIC database link from CDB2 to CDB1
*/

-- RUN THIS FROM CDB2!!!

DROP PUBLIC DATABASE LINK pdbxfer;
CREATE PUBLIC DATABASE LINK pdbxfer
    CONNECT TO c##linkup IDENTIFIED BY oracle_4U
    USING 'CDB1';

SELECT name, open_mode from v$database@pdbxfer;
```

```
SQL@CDB2> @Create_CDB2_Link.sql
DROP PUBLIC DATABASE LINK pdbxfer

ERROR at line 1:
ORA-02024: database link not found

Database link created.

PDB      Open
Name     Mode
-------- ------------
CDB1     READ WRITE
```

Next, from a new terminal window, we'll connect to the QA_HR PDB on CDB1 using an EZCONNECT connection to connect to that PDB's database service via the Listener.

NOTE: Don't forget to change the HOST string highlighted below to match the host you've been assigned:

```
$> sqlplus hr/hr@PDBME:1521/qa_hr.compute-a427312.oraclecloud.internal
```

Now, generate a workload against the HR.EMPLOYEES table to update employee salary and commission percent to random values, for a selected subset of employees.

The script that generates the DML is shown here.

```
/*
|| Script:  Generate_HR_DML.sql
|| Purpose: Updates and then reports upon salaries for all employees in
||          Department #60 in HR.EMPLOYEES
*/

UPDATE hr.employees
   SET
       salary = ROUND(DBMS_RANDOM.VALUE(1000,119999),2)
      ,commission_pct = ROUND(DBMS_RANDOM.VALUE(0.01, 0.25),2)
 WHERE department_id = 60
;

COMMIT;
```

```
SQL@CDB1> @Generate_HR_DML.sql
5 rows updated.

Commit complete.
```

Below is the script to verify the new values for the affected entries in HR.EMPLOYEES.

```
/*
|| Script:  Verify_HR_DML.sql
|| Purpose: Lists contents of HR.EMPLOYEES for Department #60
*/

SELECT last_name, salary, commission_pct
  FROM hr.employees
 WHERE department_id = 60
 ORDER BY last_name
;
```

The results below may vary a bit from what you see, but what's important is we've generated new values for the SALARY and COMMISSION_PCT columns, and thus generated transactions.

```
SQL@CDB1> @Verify_HR_DML.sql

LAST_NAME                        SALARY COMMISSION_PCT
------------------------ -------------- --------------
Austin                         94624.95            .05
Ernst                          53036.67            .08
Hunold                         10115.72            .14
Lorentz                        13484.84            .18
Pataballa                      89916.24             .1
Zlotkey                        66777.24            .22

6 rows selected.
```

Now let's initiate a "hot" migration of the QA_HR PDB on CDB1, migrating it directly to CDB2. Here is the script that we'll use to initiate that migration.

```
/*
|| Script:  Start_PDB_Relocate.sql
|| Purpose: Initiates first phase of PDB "hot" relocate from CDB1 to
CDB2
*/

-- RUN ON CDB2 !!!
-- RUN ON CDB2 !!!
-- RUN ON CDB2 !!!

CREATE PLUGGABLE DATABASE qa_hr
  FROM qa_hr@pdbxfer
    FILE_NAME_CONVERT = (

'/u01/app/oracle/oradata/CDB1/QA_HR/','/u01/app/oracle/oradata/CDB2/QA_
HR/',

'/u01/app/oracle/oradata/temp/','/u01/app/oracle/oradata/CDB2/QA_HR/'
    )
    KEYSTORE IDENTIFIED BY "IOU_Genius5"
    RELOCATE AVAILABILITY MAX;
```

Note: This operation must be started from CDB2!

```
SQL@CDB2> @Start_PDB_Relocate.sql
CREATE PLUGGABLE DATABASE qa_hr
  2     FROM qa_hr@pdbxfer
    FILE_NAME_CONVERT = (

'/u02/app/oracle/oradata/CDB1/QA_HR/','/u02/app/oracle/oradata/CDB2/QA_
HR/',

'/u04/app/oracle/oradata/temp/','/u02/app/oracle/oradata/CDB2/QA_HR/'
    )
    KEYSTORE IDENTIFIED BY "IOU_Geniu5"
    RELOCATE AVAILABILITY MAX;

Pluggable database created.
```

We can keep an eye on the progress of the hot migration through the "tailed" alert logs of both CDBs. For example, here's **CDB1's** alert log.

```
2017-09-10T15:03:07.263565-05:00
PROD_AP(6):JIT: pid 6318 requesting full stop
2017-09-10T15:03:07.266998-05:00
QA_HR(4):JIT: pid 6314 requesting full stop
2017-09-10T15:09:08.066413-05:00
QA_HR(4): AUDSYS.AUD$UNIFIED (SQL_TEXT) - CLOB populated
QA_HR(4):WARNING: Detected that PDB needs to import keys from source.
PDB can only open in restricted mode until import.
. . .
```

Next is an example from **CDB2's** alert log.

```
2017-09-10T15:09:07.342913-05:00
CREATE PLUGGABLE DATABASE qa_hr
  FROM qa_hr@pdbxfer
    FILE_NAME_CONVERT = (

'/u01/app/oracle/oradata/CDB1/QA_HR/','/u01/app/oracle/oradata/CDB2/QA_
HR/',

'/u01/app/oracle/oradata/temp/','/u01/app/oracle/oradata/CDB2/QA_HR/'
    )
    KEYSTORE IDENTIFIED BY *
    RELOCATE AVAILABILITY MAX
2017-09-10T15:09:16.164324-05:00
QA_HR(3):Endian type of dictionary set to little
*****************************************************************
Pluggable Database QA_HR with pdb id - 3 is created as UNUSABLE.
If any errors are encountered before the pdb is marked as NEW,
then the pdb must be dropped
local undo-1, localundoscn-0x00000000000000e1
*****************************************************************
2017-09-10T15:09:18.156923-05:00
Applying media recovery for pdb-4099 from SCN 1654872 to SCN 1654890
Remote log information: count-1
thr-1, seq-9, logfile-
/u01/app/oracle/fast_recovery_area/CDB1/CDB1/foreign_archivelog/QA_HR/2
017_09_10/o1_mf_1_9_2869213763_.arc, los-1611737, nxs-
18446744073709551615
QA_HR(3):Media Recovery Start
2017-09-10T15:09:18.160592-05:00
QA_HR(3):Serial Media Recovery started
2017-09-10T15:09:18.205614-05:00
```

```
QA_HR(3):Media Recovery Log
/u01/app/oracle/fast_recovery_area/CDB1/CDB1/foreign_archivelog/QA_HR/2
017_09_10/o1_mf_1_9_2869213763_.arc
2017-09-10T15:09:19.372400-05:00
QA_HR(3):Incomplete Recovery applied until change 1654890 time
09/10/2017 15:09:16
2017-09-10T15:09:19.376993-05:00
QA_HR(3):Media Recovery Complete (CDB2)
Completed: CREATE PLUGGABLE DATABASE qa_hr
  FROM qa_hr@pdbxfer
    FILE_NAME_CONVERT = (

'/u01/app/oracle/oradata/CDB1/QA_HR/','/u01/app/oracle/oradata/CDB2/QA_
HR/',

'/u01/app/oracle/oradata/temp/','/u01/app/oracle/oradata/CDB2/QA_HR/'
    )
    KEYSTORE IDENTIFIED BY *
    RELOCATE AVAILABILITY MAX
. . .
```

We can also run pdbstate.sql from both CDBs to verify the progress of this operation.

From **CDB1**:
```
SQL@CDB1> @pdbstate.sql

                    PDB Status
                 (from V$PDBS)
PDB        Open
Name       Mode
--------   ------------
DEV_AP     READ WRITE
PDB$SEED   READ ONLY
PROD_AP    READ WRITE
PROD_HR    READ WRITE
QA_HR      READ WRITE
                         PDB Status
                      (from CDB_PDBS)
PDB                             Proxy  Refresh    Rfrsh
Name       Status     Logging?  PDB?   Mode       Intvl
--------   ------     ---------  -----  --------   ------
DEV_AP     NORMAL     LOGGING    NO     NONE
PDB$SEED   NORMAL     LOGGING    NO     NONE
PROD_AP    NORMAL     LOGGING    NO     NONE
PROD_HR    NORMAL     LOGGING    NO     NONE
QA_HR      NORMAL     LOGGING    NO     NONE
```

From **CDB2**:

```
SQL@CDB2> @pdbstate.sql

              PDB Status
             (from V$PDBS)
PDB       Open
Name      Mode
--------  ------------
PDB$SEED  READ ONLY
QA_HR     MOUNTED
                        PDB Status
                       (from CDB_PDBS)
PDB                                    Proxy  Refresh  Rfrsh
Name      Status        Logging?       PDB?   Mode     Intvl
--------  ------------  ------------   -----  -------  ------
PDB$SEED  NORMAL        LOGGING        NO     NONE
QA_HR     RELOCATING    LOGGING        NO     NONE
```

While the hot migration is underway, it's still possible to perform transactions against the source PDB on CDB1. Let's update the HR.EMPLOYEES table with random values again and then commit the changes.

```
SQL@CDB1> ALTER SESSION SET CONTAINER = qa_hr;
Session altered.

SQL@CDB1> @Generate_HR_DML.sql
5 rows updated.
Commit complete.

SQL@CDB1> @Verify_HR_DML.sql

LAST_NAME                        SALARY  COMMISSION_PCT
------------------------  ------------  --------------
Austin                       94624.95             .05
Ernst                        53036.67             .08
Hunold                       10115.72             .14
Lorentz                      13484.84             .18
Pataballa                    89916.24              .1
Zlotkey                      66777.24             .22

6 rows selected.
```

To complete the hot migration, we still need to open PDB **QA_HR** in READ WRITE mode on CDB2 to complete the transition. We'll use the code in script Finish_PDB_Relocate.sql to accomplish this.

```
/*
|| Script: Finish_PDB_Relocate.sql
|| Purpose: Completes second phase of PDB "hot" relocate from CDB1 to
CDB2
*/

-- RUN ON CDB2!!!

ALTER PLUGGABLE DATABASE qa_hr OPEN READ WRITE;
```

Again, this operation must be performed from CDB2.

```
SQL@CDB2> @Finish_PDB_Relocate.sql
```

To verify the migration is complete, let's take a look at the CDBs' alert logs.

From **CDB1**:

```
. . .
2017-09-10T15:15:08.570955-05:00
QA_HR(4):JIT: pid 7539 requesting stop
QA_HR(4):KILL SESSION for sid=(37, 27190):
QA_HR(4):   Reason = PDB close immediate
QA_HR(4):   Mode = KILL HARD FORCE -/-/-
QA_HR(4):   Requestor = USER (orapid = 58, ospid = 7539, inst = 1)
QA_HR(4):   Owner = Process: USER (orapid = 62, ospid = 6430)
QA_HR(4):   Result = ORA-0
2017-09-10T15:15:09.674823-05:00
Pluggable database QA_HR closed
QA_HR(4):JIT: pid 7539 requesting stop
Pluggable database QA_HR closed
2017-09-10T15:15:13.463672-05:00
Deleted file /u01/app/oracle/oradata/CDB1/QA_HR/temp01.dbf
. . .
```

From **CDB2**:

```
. . .
2017-09-10T15:15:03.110809-05:00
ALTER PLUGGABLE DATABASE qa_hr OPEN READ WRITE
2017-09-10T15:15:05.982059-05:00
Applying media recovery for pdb-4099 from SCN 1654890 to SCN 1656464
Remote log information: count-1
thr-1, seq-9, logfile-
/u01/app/oracle/fast_recovery_area/CDB1/CDB1/foreign_archivelog/QA_HR/2
017_09_10/o1_mf_1_9_2869213763_.arc, los-1611737, nxs-
18446744073709551615
QA_HR(3):Media Recovery Start
2017-09-10T15:15:05.982899-05:00
QA_HR(3):Serial Media Recovery started
2017-09-10T15:15:06.035366-05:00
QA_HR(3):Media Recovery Log
/u01/app/oracle/fast_recovery_area/CDB1/CDB1/foreign_archivelog/QA_HR/2
017_09_10/o1_mf_1_9_2869213763_.arc
2017-09-10T15:15:07.233318-05:00
QA_HR(3):Incomplete Recovery applied until change 1656464 time
09/10/2017 15:15:03
2017-09-10T15:15:07.238514-05:00
QA_HR(3):Media Recovery Complete (CDB2)
QA_HR(3):Autotune of undo retention is turned on.
QA_HR(3):Undo initialization finished serial:0 start:34066787
end:34066787 diff:0 ms (0.0 seconds)
QA_HR(3):Database Characterset for QA_HR is AL32UTF8
. . .
QA_HR(3):Opening pdb with no Resource Manager plan active
2017-09-10T15:15:09.676175-05:00
QA_HR(3):JIT: pid 302 requesting stop
2017-09-10T15:15:11.977277-05:00
Applying media recovery for pdb-4099 from SCN 1656464 to SCN 1656522
Remote log information: count-1
thr-1, seq-9, logfile-
/u01/app/oracle/fast_recovery_area/CDB1/CDB1/foreign_archivelog/QA_HR/2
017_09_10/o1_mf_1_9_2869213763_.arc, los-1611737, nxs-
18446744073709551615
QA_HR(3):Media Recovery Start
2017-09-10T15:15:11.978031-05:00
QA_HR(3):Serial Media Recovery started
2017-09-10T15:15:12.010783-05:00
QA_HR(3):Media Recovery Log
/u01/app/oracle/fast_recovery_area/CDB1/CDB1/foreign_archivelog/QA_HR/2
017_09_10/o1_mf_1_9_2869213763_.arc
```

```
2017-09-10T15:15:13.257737-05:00
QA_HR(3):Incomplete Recovery applied until change 1656522 time
09/10/2017 15:15:09
2017-09-10T15:15:13.262985-05:00
QA_HR(3):Media Recovery Complete (CDB2)
QA_HR(3):[302] Successfully onlined Undo Tablespace 2.
QA_HR(3):Undo initialization finished serial:0 start:34072656
end:34072677 diff:21 ms (0.0 seconds)
QA_HR(3):Database Characterset for QA_HR is AL32UTF8
QA_HR(3):[302] Successfully onlined Undo Tablespace 2.
QA_HR(3):Undo initialization finished serial:0 start:34072846
end:34072883 diff:37 ms (0.0 seconds)
QA_HR(3):Deleting old file#12 from file$
QA_HR(3):Deleting old file#13 from file$
QA_HR(3):Deleting old file#14 from file$
QA_HR(3):Adding new file#9 to file$(old file#12)
QA_HR(3):Adding new file#10 to file$(old file#13)
QA_HR(3):Adding new file#11 to file$(old file#14)
QA_HR(3):Successfully created internal service qa_hr.compute-
a427312.oraclecloud.internal at open

2017-09-10T15:15:14.562296-05:00
QA_HR(3):Opening pdb with no Resource Manager plan active
Pluggable database QA_HR opened read write
Completed: ALTER PLUGGABLE DATABASE qa_hr OPEN READ WRITE
. . .
```

pdbstate.sql can also be run from both CDBs to verify the final state of the migration.

From **CDB1**:
```
SQL@CDB1> @pdbstate.sql
```

```
                    PDB Status
                  (from V$PDBS)

PDB        Open
Name       Mode
--------   ------------
DEV_AP     READ WRITE
PDB$SEED   READ ONLY
PROD_AP    READ WRITE
PROD_HR    READ WRITE
QA_HR      MOUNTED
```

```
                          PDB Status
                        (from CDB_PDBS)
PDB                                     Proxy  Refresh  Rfrsh
Name       Status       Logging?        PDB?   Mode     Intvl
--------   ----------   ------------    -----  -------  ------
DEV_AP     NORMAL       LOGGING         NO     NONE
PDB$SEED   NORMAL       LOGGING         NO     NONE
PROD_AP    NORMAL       LOGGING         NO     NONE
PROD_HR    NORMAL       LOGGING         NO     NONE
QA_HR      RELOCATED    LOGGING         NO     NONE
```

From **CDB2**:
```
SQL@CDB2> @pdbstate.sql

              PDB Status
             (from V$PDBS)
PDB        Open
Name       Mode
--------   ------------
PDB$SEED   READ ONLY
QA_HR      READ WRITE

                     PDB Status
                    (from CDB_PDBS)
PDB                               Proxy  Refresh  Rfrsh
Name       Status      Logging?   PDB?   Mode     Intvl
--------   ---------   ---------   -----  -------  ------
PDB$SEED   NORMAL      LOGGING     NO     NONE
QA_HR      NORMAL      LOGGING     NO     NONE
```

The hot migration appears to be complete. To verify, let's rerun script
verify_HR_DML.sql.

```
SQL@CDB1> @verify_HR_DML.sql
SELECT last_name, salary, commission_pct
*
ERROR at line 1:
ORA-03113: end-of-file on communication channel
Process ID: 6430
Session ID: 37 Serial number: 27190
```

This is expected behavior, because the original connection to the QA_HR PDB has
been terminated.Now, let's try to connect to QA_HR again and see which PDB we will
be routed to.

```
$> sqlplus hr/hr@PDBME:1521/qa_hr.compute-a427312.oraclecloud.internal
```

Note that the QA_HR database service has been automatically reconfigured, and all
future connections are now routed to that PDB on CDB2. To confirm, let's rerun
verify_HR_DML.sql from this newly-established session to show that the DML
executed against QA_HR on CDB1 while the hot migration was in progress, is now
reflected properly after QA_HR was moved to CDB2.

```
SQL> @verify_HR_DML.sql

LAST_NAME                    SALARY  COMMISSION_PCT
--------------------------   --------  ---------------
Austin                       94624.95             .05
Ernst                        53036.67             .08
Hunold                       10115.72             .14
Lorentz                      13484.84             .18
Pataballa                    89916.24              .1
Zlotkey                      66777.24             .22

6 rows selected.
```

Note that the results from this query match the results from the QA_HR PDB just
before the final migration was initiated.

Leveraging Refreshable PDBs

Use Case: One of our organizations wants to create a read-only version of production data stored within the PROD_AP PDB that's refreshed on a regular basis. Instead of creating a materialized view of that data, we'll simply leverage the new refreshable PDB features of Oracle Database 12.2. To satisfy these requirements, we'll establish a new PDB named RO_AP on CDB2 that will accept transactions from the PROD_AP PDB on CDB1. At the outset, RO_AP will be refreshed manually.

Let's create a new RO_AP PDB on CDB2 that will accept transactions from the PROD_AP PDB on CDB1; RO_AP will be refreshed once every **5** minutes. The statements in `Create_RO_AP.sql` will be used to accomplish this.

```
/*
|| Script:  Create_RO_AP.sql
|| Purpose: Creates new refreshable PDB named RO_AP on CDB2 that points
to
||          the PROD_AP PDB and accepts changes every five (5) minutes.
*/

-- Run from CDB2!!

CREATE PLUGGABLE DATABASE ro_ap
  FROM prod_ap@pdbxfer
  FILE_NAME_CONVERT = (

'/u01/app/oracle/oradata/CDB1/QA_HR/','/u01/app/oracle/oradata/CDB2/QA_
HR/',

'/u01/app/oracle/oradata/temp/','/u01/app/oracle/oradata/CDB2/QA_HR/'
  )
  KEYSTORE IDENTIFIED BY "IOU_Genius5"
  REFRESH MODE MANUAL;
```

```
$> . oraenv
ORACLE_SID = [oracle] ? CDB2
The Oracle base remains unchanged with value /u01/app/oracle

$> sqlplus / as sysdba
SQL*Plus: Release 12.2.0.1.0 Production on Thu Jun 15 19:07:44 2017
Copyright (c) 1982, 2016, Oracle.  All rights reserved.
Connected to:
Oracle Database 12c Enterprise Edition Release 12.2.0.1.0 - 64bit
Production

SQL@CDB2> @Create_RO_AP.sql

Pluggable database created.
```

We can keep an eye on the progress of the creation of RO_AP through the "tailed" alert log of CDB2.

```
. . .
CREATE PLUGGABLE DATABASE ro_ap
  FROM prod_ap@pdbxfer
  FILE_NAME_CONVERT = (

'/u01/app/oracle/oradata/CDB1/PROD_AP/','/u01/app/oracle/oradata/CDB2/R
O_AP/',
```

```
'/u01/app/oracle/oradata/temp/','/u01/app/oracle/oradata/CDB2/RO_AP/'
)
  KEYSTORE IDENTIFIED BY *
  REFRESH MODE MANUAL
2017-09-10T16:13:11.221000-05:00
RO_AP(5):Endian type of dictionary set to little
*******************************************************************
Pluggable Database RO_AP with pdb id - 5 is created as UNUSABLE.
If any errors are encountered before the pdb is marked as NEW,
then the pdb must be dropped
local undo-1, localundoscn-0x00000000000000e1
*******************************************************************
2017-09-10T16:13:13.829239-05:00
Applying media recovery for pdb-4099 from SCN 1659252 to SCN 1659270
Remote log information: count-1
thr-1, seq-9, logfile-
/u01/app/oracle/fast_recovery_area/CDB1/CDB1/foreign_archivelog/PROD_AP
/2017_09_10/o1_mf_1_9_2165069932_.arc, los-1611737, nxs-
18446744073709551615
RO_AP(5):Media Recovery Start
2017-09-10T16:13:13.833400-05:00
RO_AP(5):Serial Media Recovery started
2017-09-10T16:13:13.897589-05:00
RO_AP(5):Media Recovery Log
/u01/app/oracle/fast_recovery_area/CDB1/CDB1/foreign_archivelog/PROD_AP
/2017_09_10/o1_mf_1_9_2165069932_.arc
2017-09-10T16:13:15.099665-05:00
RO_AP(5):Incomplete Recovery applied until change 1659270 time
09/10/2017 16:13:11
2017-09-10T16:13:15.104385-05:00
RO_AP(5):Media Recovery Complete (CDB2)
Completed: CREATE PLUGGABLE DATABASE ro_ap
  FROM prod_ap@pdbxfer
  FILE_NAME_CONVERT = (

'/u01/app/oracle/oradata/CDB1/PROD_AP/','/u01/app/oracle/oradata/CDB2/R
O_AP/',

'/u01/app/oracle/oradata/temp/','/u01/app/oracle/oradata/CDB2/RO_AP/'
)
  KEYSTORE IDENTIFIED BY *
  REFRESH MODE MANUAL
. . .
```

We can also run **pdbstate.sql** from CDB2 to confirm it state.

```
SQL@CDB2> @pdbstate.sql

            PDB Status
         (from V$PDBS)
PDB       Open
Name      Mode
--------  ------------
PDB$SEED  READ ONLY
RO_AP     MOUNTED


                  PDB Status
               (from CDB_PDBS)

PDB                               Proxy Refresh  Rfrsh
Name      Status       Logging?   PDB?  Mode     Intvl
--------  -----------  ---------- ----- -------- ------
PDB$SEED  NORMAL       LOGGING    NO    NONE
RO_AP     REFRESHING   LOGGING    NO    MANUAL
```

Now that the RO_AP refreshable PDB has been established, let's generate some transactions against PROD_AP on CDB1. We'll use the code in script Generate_AP_DML.sql to call AP.PKG_LOAD_GENERATOR to add some random, new entries to the AP.INVOICES and AP.INVOICE_ITEMS tables and commit those changes.

```
|| Script:  Generate_AP_DML.sql
|| Purpose: Generates 25 new invoices and related invoice items on
PROD_AP.
*/

-----
-- Run from CDB1:
-----
BEGIN

    AP.PKG_LOAD_GENERATOR.RandomDML(25);

    COMMIT;

EXCEPTION
    WHEN OTHERS THEN
        BEGIN
            DBMS_OUTPUT.PUT_LINE('Unexpected error during transaction
generation!!');
            ROLLBACK;
        END;

END;
/
```

```
$>sqlplus / as sysdba
. . .
SQL@CDB1> ALTER SESSION SET CONTAINER = PROD_AP;

Session altered.

SQL@CDB1> @Generate_AP_DML.sql

Commit complete.
```

To view the results of these transactions against PROD_AP, let's run script Verify_AP_DML.sql on CDB1.

```
/*
|| Script:  Verify_AP_DML.sql
|| Purpose: Verifies current state of AP tables within PDBs.
*/
COL taxable_ind FORMAT A01              HEADING "T|X|B|L"
COL itm_cnt     FORMAT 99999            HEADING "Item|Count"
COL tot_bal     FORMAT 99,999,999.99    HEADING "Total|Amount"
TTITLE "Invoice Items Verification"
SELECT
        taxable_ind
      ,COUNT(line_item_nbr) itm_cnt
      ,SUM(extended_amt) tot_bal
  FROM ap.invoice_items
 GROUP BY taxable_ind
 ORDER BY taxable_ind;
TTITLE OFF
```

```
SQL@CDB1> @Verify_AP_DML.sql
               Invoice Items Verification
T
X
B    Item          Total
L    Count         Amount
-   ------    --------------
N  |  875     1,027,873.00 |
Y  | 4000     6,583,790.50 |
```

Now let's open RO_AP on CDB2 in **READ ONLY** mode and see if the transactions from PROD_AP have been propagated there.

```
SQL@CDB2> ALTER PLUGGABLE DATABASE ro_ap OPEN READ ONLY;

Pluggable database altered.

SQL@CDB2> @pdbstate.sql

                 PDB Status
               (from V$PDBS)

PDB        Open
Name       Mode
--------   ------------
RO_AP      READ ONLY

                    PDB Status
                  (from CDB_PDBS)

PDB                                Proxy Refresh   Rfrsh
Name       Status       Logging?   PDB?  Mode      Intvl
--------   ------------ ---------- ----- --------  ------
RO_AP      REFRESHING   LOGGING    NO    MANUAL

SQL@CDB2> ALTER SESSION SET CONTAINER = RO_AP;
Session altered.

SQL@CDB2> @Verify_AP_DML.sql
               Invoice Items Verification
T
X
B    Item          Total
L    Count         Amount
-   ------    --------------
N  |  700      896,882.00 |
Y  | 3200     5,334,977.00 |
```

This is actually exactly what we expected – RO_AP will not accept any transactions from PROD_AP until the refreshable PDB is first closed and then refreshed.

Now once again let's open RO_AP on CDB2 in **READ ONLY** mode and see if the transactions from PROD_AP have been propagated there.

```
SQL@CDB2> ALTER SESSION SET CONTAINER = CDB$ROOT;
Session altered.

SQL@CDB2> ALTER PLUGGABLE DATABASE ro_ap CLOSE;
Pluggable database altered.
```

```
SQL@CDB2> ALTER SESSION SET CONTAINER = RO_AP;
Session altered.

SQL@CDB2> ALTER PLUGGABLE DATABASE ro_ap REFRESH;
Pluggable database altered.

SQL@CDB2> ALTER PLUGGABLE DATABASE ro_ap OPEN READ ONLY;
Pluggable database altered.
```

CDB2's "tailed" alert log show the results of these commands.

```
. . .
ALTER PLUGGABLE DATABASE ro_ap CLOSE
2017-09-10T16:28:19.607053-05:00
RO_AP(5):JIT: pid 12353 requesting stop
Pluggable database RO_AP closed
Completed: ALTER PLUGGABLE DATABASE ro_ap CLOSE
2017-09-10T16:28:39.695578-05:00
RO_AP(5):ALTER PLUGGABLE DATABASE ro_ap REFRESH
2017-09-10T16:28:40.922710-05:00
Applying media recovery for pdb-4099 from SCN 1659270 to SCN 1661204
Remote log information: count-1
thr-1, seq-9, logfile-
/u01/app/oracle/fast_recovery_area/CDB1/CDB1/foreign_archivelog/PROD_AP
/2017_09_10/o1_mf_1_9_2165069932_.arc, los-1611737, nxs-
18446744073709551615
RO_AP(5):Media Recovery Start
2017-09-10T16:28:40.923084-05:00
RO_AP(5):Serial Media Recovery started
2017-09-10T16:28:40.972543-05:00
RO_AP(5):Media Recovery Log
/u01/app/oracle/fast_recovery_area/CDB1/CDB1/foreign_archivelog/PROD_AP
/2017_09_10/o1_mf_1_9_2165069932_.arc
2017-09-10T16:28:42.404846-05:00
RO_AP(5):Incomplete Recovery applied until change 1661204 time
09/10/2017 16:28:40
2017-09-10T16:28:42.409753-05:00
RO_AP(5):Media Recovery Complete (CDB2)
RO_AP(5):Completed: ALTER PLUGGABLE DATABASE ro_ap REFRESH
2017-09-10T16:29:09.070136-05:00
RO_AP(5):ALTER PLUGGABLE DATABASE ro_ap OPEN READ ONLY
RO_AP(5):Autotune of undo retention is turned on.
2017-09-10T16:29:09.149397-05:00
RO_AP(5):Endian type of dictionary set to little
RO_AP(5):Undo initialization finished serial:0 start:38508603
end:38508603 diff:0 ms (0.0 seconds)
RO_AP(5):Database Characterset for RO_AP is AL32UTF8
. . .
RO_AP(5):Opening pdb with no Resource Manager plan active
Pluggable database RO_AP opened read only
RO_AP(5):Completed: ALTER PLUGGABLE DATABASE ro_ap OPEN READ ONLY
. . .
```

```
SQL@CDB2> ALTER SESSION SET CONTAINER = RO_AP;
Session altered.

SQL@CDB2> @Verify_AP_DML.sql
                    Invoice Items Verification
T
X
B     Item           Total
L    Count          Amount
-  ------  ---------------
N     875    1,027,873.00
Y    4000    6,583,790.50
```

We can also change the frequency of the refresh requests from RO_AP to PROD_AP; even though this will have no immediate impact on the state of the data in RO_AP until it is first closed and then re-opened.

```
SQL@CDB2> ALTER SESSION SET CONTAINER = RO_AP;
Session altered.

SQL@CDB2> ALTER PLUGGABLE DATABASE ro_ap REFRESH MODE EVERY 5 MINUTES;
Pluggable database altered.
```

To confirm the change, let's run **pdbstate.sql** from CDB2.

```
SQL@CDB2> @pdbstate.sql
                          PDB Status
                        (from CDB_PDBS)

PDB                                   Proxy Refresh  Rfrsh
Name       Status      Logging?       PDB?  Mode     Intvl
---------- ----------- -------------- ----- -------- ------
PDB$SEED   NORMAL      LOGGING        NO    NONE
RO_AP      REFRESHING  LOGGING        NO    AUTO          5
```

To complete this demonstration, let's first generate some new transactions on **PROD_AP** on **CDB1** and then capture the results.

```
$>sqlplus / as sysdba
. . .

SQL@CDB1> ALTER SESSION SET CONTAINER = PROD_AP;

Session altered.

SQL@CDB1> @Generate_AP_DML.sql

Commit complete.

SQL@CDB2> @Verify_AP_DML.sql

                        Invoice Items Verification

T
X
B    Item         Total
L    Count        Amount
-   ------    --------------
N    1050      1,158,864.00
Y    4800      7,832,604.00
```

Now we'll wait at least five minutes until CDB2's alert log shows the automatic request for data refresh from PROD_AP to RO_AP.

```
. . .
2017-06-18T16:34:48.443928-05:00
RO_AP(3):alter pluggable database refresh
RO_AP(3):Completed: alter pluggable database refresh
2017-06-18T16:39:47.643464-05:00
RO_AP(3):alter pluggable database refresh
RO_AP(3):Completed: alter pluggable database refresh
```

```
2017-06-18T16:44:09.566752-05:00
RO_AP(3):alter pluggable database refresh
RO_AP(3):Completed: alter pluggable database refresh
. . .
```

Let's close and reopen RO_AP on CDB2 to see the end results. You shouldn't have to reissue the ALTER PLUGGABLE DATABASE <pdb_name> REFRESH; command to request a refresh of PROD_AP's transactions against RO_AP, but it doesn't hurt to issue it.

```
SQL@CDB2> ALTER SESSION SET CONTAINER = CDB$ROOT;
Session altered.

SQL@CDB2> ALTER PLUGGABLE DATABASE ro_ap CLOSE;
Pluggable database altered.

SQL@CDB2> ALTER SESSION SET CONTAINER = RO_AP;
Session altered.

SQL@CDB2> ALTER PLUGGABLE DATABASE ro_ap REFRESH;
Pluggable database altered.

SQL@CDB2> ALTER PLUGGABLE DATABASE ro_ap OPEN READ ONLY;
Pluggable database altered.

SQL@CDB2> ALTER SESSION SET CONTAINER = RO_AP;
Session altered.

SQL@CDB2> @Verify_AP_DML.sql
```

Did you receive an error while attempting to query the contents of RO_AP? If so, that's by design. Since the pluggable database was closed, its corresponding TDE keystore closed automatically as well.

```
SQL@CDB2> @Verify_AP_DML.sql
   FROM ap.invoice_items
         *
ERROR at line 5:
ORA-28365: wallet is not open
```

It's now necessary to first reopen that PDB's TDE encryption wallet before proceeding. The good news is that this is easily accomplished with a simple command.

```
SQL@CDB2> ADMINISTER KEY MANAGEMENT SET KEYSTORE OPEN
          IDENTIFIED BY "IOU_Geniu5" CONTAINER = CURRENT;
Session altered.

SQL@CDB2> @Verify_AP_DML.sql
                         Invoice Items Verification
T
X
B    Item           Total
L    Count          Amount
-    ------   --------------
N    1050     1,158,864.00
Y    4800     7,832,604.00
```

Leveraging Proxy PDBs

Use Case #1: One of our organizations has the need to move a PDB from one data center to another data center. An outage window cannot be locked down to change all the application connections, as too many application servers are connecting to the database. Location transparency must also be provided for this database,d even though it has moved to another data center.

Use Case #2: We want to move our PDB to Oracle Cloud and create a proxy connection from on-premise to Oracle Cloud so that the applications do not have to be modified. The applications cannot be moved yet, we still want to keep them on-premise for a while, until we are more comfortable with the ports required to be punched to Oracle Cloud to all the application servers.

Moving the enterprise to the cloud or another data center does not happen overnight. Most likely, it will be a journey and a process that occurs over time. Often, we move one database or application at a time. As part of the migration, we often miss important components like connect strings or database links that can cause a production outage. With the proxy PDB, we can move a PDB from one data center to another or to Oracle Cloud, and then create a proxy PDB that references the original PDB that we just moved. In essence, the proxy PDB becomes a pointer to the referenced PDB. The beauty with the proxy PDB is that unlike database links, we can perform all DDL and DML as if we were performing the transactions natively to the referenced PDB.

To create a Proxy PDB, we must first be connected to the root container (CDB$ROOT) of the database. From that root container, we must create a database link that references the remote database. The database link must be created from the root CDB that will house the proxy PDB and can connect to either:

- the root of the remote CDB
- remote referenced PDB

We have two options when it comes to the user account that the database link connects with. The database link can point to either a common user in the referenced CDB root container or to a common/local user in the referenced PDB. The database link is initially required to create the Proxy PDB but shortly after the PDB is created, the database link is no longer used. Subsequently, the Proxy PDB communicates directly with the referenced PDB.

Once the database link is created, we can create the Proxy PDB with the CREATE PLUGGABLE DATABASE command with the AS PROXY clause.

```
$> sqlplus / as sysdba

SQL> CREATE PLUGGABLE DATABASE my_proxy_pdb1
     AS PROXY
     FROM pdb5@clone_link;

ALTER PLUGGABLE DATABASE my_proxy_pdb1 OPEN;
```

Internally, Oracle copies the SYSTEM, SYSAUX, TEMP, and UNDO tablespaces over the network to the local instance; Oracle will also keep these tablespaces synchronized. File name conversion considerations still persist since it is still a clone in practical purposes.

Oracle Managed Files (OMF) should be considered for simplification and standardization even for Proxy PDBs, so that we do not have to worry about FILE_NAME_CONVERT or PDB_FILE_NAME_CONVERT.

In order to create Proxy PDBs, there's numerous prerequisites that have to be satisfied. Obviously, you must have the CREATE PLUGGABLE DATABASE system privilege in the root CDB where the Proxy PDB is being created. The referenced PDB must be in archivelog mode and have localized undo; also it must be open in read/write mode at the time of Proxy DB creation.

Next, connect to the newly created Proxy PDB, my_proxy_pdb1 database, and perform DDL operations that you cannot perform over the traditional database links.

```
SQL> CONN sys@my_proxy_pdb1 AS SYSDBA

SQL>CREATE TABLESPACE data_p1 AUTOEXTEND ON NEXT 10M;

SQL> CREATE USER trax_owner_p1 IDENTIFIED BY viscosity
     DEFAULT TABLESPACE data_p1
     QUOTA UNLIMITED ON data_p1;

SQL> GRANT DBA to trax_owner_p1;
```

It is important to note that while SYSTEM, SYSAUX, TEMP, and UNDO reside locally where the Proxy PDB is created, other tablespaces reside in the referenced instance location; the data_p1 datafiles will be created on the remote referenced PDB.

SQL statements executed on the proxy PDB are sent to and executed in the referenced PDB. Results of the query are returned to the proxy PDB. As DDL, DML, and SELECT statements executed on the Proxy PDB, querys are sent to the referenced PDB for execution. The results are passed back to the proxy PDB. Two commands are exception to the rule. When the ALTER PLUGGABLE DATABASE and ALTER DATABASE commands are executed on the Proxy PDB, they are not sent to the referenced PDB for execution.

Dictionary Views

Proxy PDBs identity can be found in the the V$PDBS and CDB_PDBS dictionary views. From the V$PDBS view, we can issue the following SQL statement to identify if the PDB is a Proxy PDB.

```
SELECT name, proxy_pdb
```

```
FROM    v$pdbs;
```

We can also query the CDB_PDBS view.

```
SELECT  pdb_name, is_proxy_pdb
FROM    cdb_pdbs;
```

To obtain information about connection details for the referenced PDB, query the
V$PROXY_PDB_TARGETS view.

```
COLUMN  target_host FORMAT A30
COLUMN  target_service FORMAT A30
COLUMN  target_user FORMAT A30

SELECT  con_id,
        target_port,
        target_host,
        target_service,
        target_user
FROM    v$proxy_pdb_targets;
```

We can also create a Proxy PDB in a CDB root that is based on a referenced

PDB in an application container.

---

7. DBaaS Backup and Recovery

Even though we are operating within an OPC DBaaS environment, doesn't mean we can ignore the implementation of a suitable backup and recovery strategy for our CDBs and PDBs. This chapter will therefore focus on best practices for backing up, restoring, and recovering CDBs and PDBs within DBaaS. A large part of this discussion will be on a brand-new feature in Oracle Database 12cR2: the ability to perform FLASHBACK PLUGGABLE DATABASE operations against an individual PDB without having to recover the entire CDB.

Note: We strongly recommend that you perform RMAN backups at the CDB level. Unless you have special considerations for performing backups at the PDB level, you should as a standard, perform backups for the entire CDB.

To perform a full backup at the CDB level, you can use the following RMAN script with minimum modifications.

```
#Script: rman2disk.sql
run
{
CONFIGURE DEVICE TYPE DISK PARALLELISM 4 BACKUP TYPE TO BACKUPSET;

crosscheck copy of controlfile;
delete noprompt expired copy of controlfile;

crosscheck backup;
delete noprompt expired backup;

crosscheck archivelog all;
delete noprompt expired archivelog all;

delete noprompt obsolete;

backup as backupset incremental level ###_BACKUP_LEVEL_###
tag=###_ORACLE_SID_###_bkup_###_BACKUP_LEVEL_###_###_DATE_### filesperset 1 format
'/u01/app/oracle/admin/###_ORACLE_SID_###/bkups/%d.%s.%p.%t.L###_BACKUP_LEVEL_###.DB'
(database) ;

###_sqlspfile_### "create
pfile=''/u01/app/oracle/admin/###_ORACLE_SID_###/bkups/init_###_ORACLE_SID_###_###_DATE_
###.ora'' from spfile";
sql "alter system archive log current";
sql "alter system switch logfile";
sql "alter system switch logfile";


sql "alter database backup controlfile to trace";
#sql "alter database backup controlfile to
''/u01/app/oracle/admin/###_ORACLE_SID_###/bkups/control01_###_ORACLE_SID_###_###_DATE_#
##.ctl.bkup''";

backup as backupset format
'/u01/app/oracle/admin/###_ORACLE_SID_###/bkups/%d.%s.%p.%t.A' skip inaccessible
(archivelog all not backed up 2 times);
backup tag=###_ORACLE_SID_###_CTL_###_DATE_### format
'/u01/app/oracle/admin/###_ORACLE_SID_###/bkups/%d.%s.%p.%t.CTL' (current controlfile);

delete noprompt archivelog until time 'sysdate - ###_NUMBER_OF_DAYS_TO_RETAIN_###'
backed up 2 times to device type disk;
}
```

The ###_[VAR]_XXX parameters are substituted from input parameters passed to the `rman2disk.ksh` script that you can download from http://dbaexpert.com/rman2disk.ksh. To perform a full level 0 backup, execute the shell script with the following parameters.

```
rman2disk.ksh -d DATABASE -l 0 -c catalog >
/tmp/rman2disk_DATABASE.0.log 2>&1
```

Let's break down the arguments in this command:

- **-d** specifies the name of the database that is defined in `/etc/oratab`.
- **-l** specifies whether it will be an incremental level 0 backup (if set to zero) or an incremental level 1 backup (if set to 1).
- **-c** specifies whether the RMAN repository will be used to store the backup metadata and log information.
- Lastly, the script also accepts a **-z** (**y**)es option if you want to compress your RMAN backups.

As with any rule of performing backups at the CDB level, there are always exceptions. The more you consolidate, the more reasons you will find to isolate backups at the PDB level. For example, the following use case may occur on a routine basis: You want to perform a backup of just a single PDB, because you are running a major code release for an application, and the schemas and back-end PL/SQL application logic will be modified quite a bit.

The easiest way to perform a level 0 full backup is by simply issuing the one-liner command to backup the database and archive logs.

```
BACKUP DATABASE PLUS ARCHIVELOG;
```

Note: We strongly recommend that you turn on automatic backup of control files. If you are not using a RMAN recovery catalog, it is recommended that you enable controlfile auto-backups:

CONFIGURE CONTROLFILE AUTOBACKUP ON;

PDB Level RMAN Backup

In this example, we will back up a single PDB named **ANITASPDB2** using RMAN. As you can see, backing up a pluggable database is extremely simple; the only essential difference is the addition of the **PLUGGABLE** keyword.

```
$> rman target /

Recovery Manager: Release 12.2.0.1.0 - Production on Tue Jul 11 17:53:09 2017
Copyright (c) 1982, 2017, Oracle and/or its affiliates.  All rights reserved.
connected to target database: ANITASDB (DBID=2245464683)
```

```
RMAN> backup pluggable database ANITASPDB2;
Starting backup at 11-JUL-17
using target database control file instead of recovery catalog
allocated channel: ORA_DISK_1
channel ORA_DISK_1: SID=110 device type=DISK
channel ORA_DISK_1: starting full datafile backup set
channel ORA_DISK_1: specifying datafile(s) in backup set
input datafile file number=00047
name=/u01/app/oracle/oradata/JOHNSPDB2/ANITASDB/4F20CED2900D14D4E055000000000001/datafil
e/o1_mf_sysaux_dlcz6omj_.dbf
input datafile file number=00046
name=/u01/app/oracle/oradata/JOHNSPDB2/ANITASDB/4F20CED2900D14D4E055000000000001/datafil
e/o1_mf_system_dlcz6om3_.dbf
input datafile file number=00048
name=/u01/app/oracle/oradata/JOHNSPDB2/ANITASDB/4F20CED2900D14D4E055000000000001/datafil
e/o1_mf_undotbs1_dlcz6omk_.dbf
input datafile file number=00049
name=/u01/app/oracle/oradata/JOHNSPDB2/ANITASDB/4F20CED2900D14D4E055000000000001/datafil
e/o1_mf_users_dlcz6omm_.dbf
channel ORA_DISK_1: starting piece 1 at 11-JUL-17
channel ORA_DISK_1: finished piece 1 at 11-JUL-17
piece
handle=/u01/app/oracle/fast_recovery_area/ANITASDB/ANITASDB/4F20CED2900D14D4E05500000000
0001/backupset/2017_07_11/o1_mf_nnndf_TAG20170711T175323_dpboq46z_.bkp
tag=TAG20170711T175323 comment=NONE
channel ORA_DISK_1: backup set complete, elapsed time: 00:00:36
Finished backup at 11-JUL-17
Starting Control File and SPFILE Autobackup at 11-JUL-17
piece
handle=/u01/app/oracle/fast_recovery_area/ANITASDB/ANITASDB/autobackup/2017_07_11/o1_mf_
s_949082039_dpbor8h1_.bkp comment=NONE
Finished Control File and SPFILE Autobackup at 11-JUL-17
```

You can back up multiple PDBs at the same time by listing the PDBs in a comma-delimited list. For example, to backup the **OLTPROD** and **DSSPROD** at the same time, use the below command.

```
RMAN> backup pluggable database OLTPROD, DSSPROD;
```

PDB Recovery After Loss of a Datafile

The following steps document how a PDB is recovered from the loss of a datafile. Before we begin, we will list out the datafiles for the pluggable database:

```
ORACLE_SID = [oracle] ? ANITASDB

The Oracle base has been set to /u01/app/oracle
$> sqlplus / as sysdba
SQL*Plus: Release 12.2.0.1.0 Production on Tue Jul 11 17:55:23 2017
Copyright (c) 1982, 2016, Oracle. All rights reserved.
Connected to:
Oracle Database 12c Enterprise Edition Release 12.2.0.1.0 - 64bit
Production

SQL> alter session set container = ANITASPDB2;

Session altered.

SQL> select file_name from dba_data_files;

FILE_NAME
----------------------------------------------------------------
/u01/app/oracle/oradata/JOHNSPDB2/ANITASDB/4F20CED2900D14D4E055000000000001/datafile/o1_
mf_system_dlcz6om3_.dbf
/u01/app/oracle/oradata/JOHNSPDB2/ANITASDB/4F20CED2900D14D4E055000000000001/datafile/o1_
mf_sysaux_dlcz6omj_.dbf
/u01/app/oracle/oradata/JOHNSPDB2/ANITASDB/4F20CED2900D14D4E055000000000001/datafile/o1_
mf_undotbs1_dlcz6omk_.dbf
/u01/app/oracle/oradata/JOHNSPDB2/ANITASDB/4F20CED2900D14D4E055000000000001/datafile/o1_
mf_users_dlcz6omm_.dbf
```

```
SQL> show pdbs

    CON_ID CON_NAME                                  OPEN MODE  RESTRICTED
---------- ------------------------------           ---------- ----------
         6 ANITASPDB2                                READ WRITE NO
```

To imitate a lost datafile scenario, let's rename (via mv) a datafile from the PDB. In the example below, we will rename the o1_mf_users_d1cz6omm_.dbf file to initiate a database failure.

```
$> cd /u01/app/oracle/oradata/JOHNSPDB2/ANITASDB
$> cd 4F20CED2900D14D4E055000000000001/datafile
$> mv o1_mf_users_d1cz6omm_.dbf user.bkp
```

Now, let's check on the damage. We immediately encounter the ORA-01116 and ORA-01110 errors followed by an OS Linux x86_64 error.

```
$> sqlplus / as sysdba
SQL*Plus: Release 12.2.0.1.0 Production on Tue Jul 11 17:59:06 2017
Copyright (c) 1982, 2016, Oracle.  All rights reserved.
Connected to:
Oracle Database 12c Enterprise Edition Release 12.2.0.1.0 - 64bit
Production

SQL> alter session set container=ANITASPDB2;

Session altered.

SQL> select * from RAHEEM.ABC;
select * from RAHEEM.ABC
                     *
ERROR at line 1:
ORA-01116: error in opening database file 49
ORA-01110: data file 49:
'/u01/app/oracle/oradata/JOHNSPDB2/ANITASDB/4F20CED2900D14D4E055000000000001/dat
afile/o1_mf_users_d1cz6omm_.dbf'
ORA-27041: unable to open file
Linux-x86_64 Error: 2: No such file or directory
Additional information: 3
```

If we try to reopen this PDB, we'll immediately encounter the dreaded ORA-01113 database file needs recovery message.

```
SQL> alter pluggable database ANITASPDB2 close;
Pluggable database altered.

SQL> alter pluggable database ANITASPDB2 open;
alter pluggable database ANITASPDB2 open
*
ERROR at line 1:
ORA-01113: file 49 needs media recovery
ORA-01110: data file 49:
'/u01/app/oracle/oradata/ANITASDB/4F20CED2900D14D4E055000000000001/datafile/o1_m
f_users_dpbp6c79_.dbf'
```

Restoring a Pluggable Database from RMAN Backup

Instead of restoring the PDB's datafiles *individually*, we will restore the database from backup. Prior to attempting to restore the PDB, please make sure that the PDB has been closed (using the ALTER PLUGGABLE DATABASE ANITAPDB2 CLOSE; command);

otherwise, you will encounter an **ORA-19573** error and related error message(s).

```
RMAN> restore pluggable database ANITASPDB2;
Starting restore at 11-JUL-17
using channel ORA_DISK_1
channel ORA_DISK_1: starting datafile backup set restore
channel ORA_DISK_1: specifying datafile(s) to restore from backup set
channel ORA_DISK_1: restoring datafile 00046 to
/u01/app/oracle/oradata/JOHNSPDB2/ANITASDB/4F20CED2900D14D4E055000000000001/datafile/o1_
mf_system_dlcz6om3_.dbf
channel ORA_DISK_1: restoring datafile 00047 to
/u01/app/oracle/oradata/JOHNSPDB2/ANITASDB/4F20CED2900D14D4E055000000000001/datafile/o1_
mf_sysaux_dlcz6omj_.dbf
channel ORA_DISK_1: restoring datafile 00048 to
/u01/app/oracle/oradata/JOHNSPDB2/ANITASDB/4F20CED2900D14D4E055000000000001/datafile/o1_
mf_undotbs1_dlcz6omk_.dbf
channel ORA_DISK_1: restoring datafile 00049 to
/u01/app/oracle/oradata/JOHNSPDB2/ANITASDB/4F20CED2900D14D4E055000000000001/datafile/o1_
mf_users_dlcz6omm_.dbf
channel ORA_DISK_1: reading from backup piece
/u01/app/oracle/fast_recovery_area/ANITASDB/ANITASDB/4F20CED2900D14D4E055000000000001/ba
ckupset/2017_07_11/o1_mf_nnndf_TAG20170711T175323_dpboq46z_.bkp
RMAN-00571: ===========================================================
RMAN-00569: =============== ERROR MESSAGE STACK FOLLOWS ===============
RMAN-00571: ===========================================================
RMAN-03002: failure of restore command at 07/11/2017 18:00:56
ORA-19870: error while restoring backup piece
/u01/app/oracle/fast_recovery_area/ANITASDB/ANITASDB/4F20CED2900D14D4E055000000000001/ba
ckupset/2017_07_11/o1_mf_nnndf_TAG20170711T175323_dpboq46z_.bkp
ORA-19573: cannot obtain exclusive enqueue for datafile 47
ORA-45909: restore, recover or block media recovery may be in progress
```

Let's try the restore of the PDB again after closing the PDB.

```
RMAN> restore pluggable database ANITASPDB2;

Starting restore at 11-JUL-17
using channel ORA_DISK_1

channel ORA_DISK_1: starting datafile backup set restore
channel ORA_DISK_1: specifying datafile(s) to restore from backup set
channel ORA_DISK_1: restoring datafile 00046 to
/u01/app/oracle/oradata/JOHNSPDB2/ANITASDB/4F20CED2900D14D4E055000000000001/datafile/o1_
mf_system_dlcz6om3_.dbf
channel ORA_DISK_1: restoring datafile 00047 to
/u01/app/oracle/oradata/JOHNSPDB2/ANITASDB/4F20CED2900D14D4E055000000000001/datafile/o1_
mf_sysaux_dlcz6omj_.dbf
channel ORA_DISK_1: restoring datafile 00048 to
/u01/app/oracle/oradata/JOHNSPDB2/ANITASDB/4F20CED2900D14D4E055000000000001/datafile/o1_
mf_undotbs1_dlcz6omk_.dbf
channel ORA_DISK_1: restoring datafile 00049 to
/u01/app/oracle/oradata/JOHNSPDB2/ANITASDB/4F20CED2900D14D4E055000000000001/datafile/o1_
mf_users_dlcz6omm_.dbf
channel ORA_DISK_1: reading from backup piece
/u01/app/oracle/fast_recovery_area/ANITASDB/ANITASDB/4F20CED2900D14D4E055000000000001/ba
ckupset/2017_07_11/o1_mf_nnndf_TAG20170711T175323_dpboq46z_.bkp
channel ORA_DISK_1: piece
handle=/u01/app/oracle/fast_recovery_area/ANITASDB/ANITASDB/4F20CED2900D14D4E05500000000
0001/backupset/2017_07_11/o1_mf_nnndf_TAG20170711T175323_dpboq46z_.bkp
tag=TAG20170711T175323
channel ORA_DISK_1: restored backup piece 1
channel ORA_DISK_1: restore complete, elapsed time: 00:00:35
Finished restore at 11-JUL-17
```

Point-In-Time Recovery of the PDB based on SCN

In this example, we will obtain the SCN for the point-in-time recovery of the PDB. Let's start by determining the SCN from the last RMAN backup using the **LIST BACKUP** command.

```
$> rman target /

Recovery Manager: Release 12.2.0.1.0 - Production on Tue Jul 11
18:44:57 2017

Copyright (c) 1982, 2017, Oracle and/or its affiliates. All rights
reserved.

connected to target database: ANITASDB (DBID=2245464683)

RMAN> list backup of database;
using target database control file instead of recovery catalog

List of Backup Sets
===================
BS Key  Type LV Size       Device Type Elapsed Time Completion Time
------- ---- -- ---------- ----------- ------------ ---------------
20      Full    602.87M    DISK        00:00:30     11-JUL-17
        BP Key: 20   Status: AVAILABLE  Compressed: NO  Tag: TAG20170711T175323
        Piece Name:
/u01/app/oracle/fast_recovery_area/ANITASDB/ANITASDB/4F20CED2900D14D4E055000000000001/ba
ckupset/2017_07_11/o1_mf_nnndf_TAG20170711T175323_dpboq46z_.bkp
   List of Datafiles in backup set 20
   Container ID: 6, PDB Name: ANITASPDB2
   File LV Type Ckp SCN    Ckp Time   Abs Fuz SCN Sparse Name
   ---- -- ---- ---------- ---------- ----------- ------ ----
   46      Full 10952577   11-JUL-17              NO
/u01/app/oracle/oradata/JOHNSPDB2/ANITASDB/4F20CED2900D14D4E055000000000001/datafile/o1_
mf_system_d1cz6om3_.dbf
   47      Full 10952577   11-JUL-17              NO
/u01/app/oracle/oradata/JOHNSPDB2/ANITASDB/4F20CED2900D14D4E055000000000001/datafile/o1_
mf_sysaux_d1cz6omj_.dbf
   48      Full 10952577   11-JUL-17              NO
/u01/app/oracle/oradata/JOHNSPDB2/ANITASDB/4F20CED2900D14D4E055000000000001/datafile/o1_
mf_undotbs1_d1cz6omk_.dbf
   49      Full 10952577   11-JUL-17              NO
/u01/app/oracle/oradata/ANITASDB/4F20CED2900D14D4E055000000000001/datafile/o1_mf_users_d
pbp6c79_.dbf
```

We will perform a recovery of the PDB based on the SCN of 10952577. For Point-In-Time recovery, Oracle 12.2 builds an auxiliary instance. Recall that you have an option to specify the PATH for the datafiles of auxiliary instance. Script recover_pdb.rman shown below contains the command script we'll leverage for the recovery operation.

```
# Script: recover_pdb.man
RMAN> run {
set until scn 10952577;
recover pluggable database ANITASPDB2;
}
```

The output below demonstrates the SCN based Point-in-time Recovery of a Pluggable Database.

```
$> rman target /

Recovery Manager: Release 12.2.0.1.0 - Production on Tue Jul 11
18:49:04 2017

Copyright (c) 1982, 2017, Oracle and/or its affiliates. All rights
reserved.

connected to target database: ANITASDB (DBID=2245464683)

RMAN> @recover_pdb.rman
```

```
RMAN> run {
2> set until scn 10952577;
3> recover pluggable database ANITASPDB2;
4> }
executing command: SET until clause

Starting recover at 11-JUL-17
using target database control file instead of recovery catalog
current log archived
allocated channel: ORA_DISK_1
channel ORA_DISK_1: SID=67 device type=DISK
RMAN-05026: warning: presuming following set of tablespaces applies to specified point-
in-time

List of tablespaces expected to have UNDO segments
Tablespace SYSTEM
Tablespace UNDOTBS1

Creating automatic instance, with SID='hlDp'

initialization parameters used for automatic instance:
db_name=ANITASDB
db_unique_name=hlDp_pitr_ANITASPDB2_ANITASDB
compatible=12.2.0
db_block_size=8192
db_files=200
diagnostic_dest=/u01/app/oracle
_system_trig_enabled=FALSE
sga_target=696M
processes=200
#No auxiliary destination in use
enable_pluggable_database=true
_clone_one_pdb_recovery=true
control_files=/u01/app/oracle/fast_recovery_area/ANITASDB/ANITASDB/controlfile/o1_mf_dpb
rzx1q_.ctl
#No auxiliary parameter file used


starting up automatic instance ANITASDB

Oracle instance started

Total System Global Area    729808896 bytes

Fixed Size                    8797056 bytes
Variable Size               205522048 bytes
Database Buffers            511705088 bytes
Redo Buffers                  3784704 bytes
Automatic instance created

contents of Memory Script:
{
# set requested point in time
set until  scn 10952577;
# restore the controlfile
restore clone controlfile;

# mount the controlfile
sql clone 'alter database mount clone database';
}
executing Memory Script

executing command: SET until clause

Starting restore at 11-JUL-17
allocated channel: ORA_AUX_DISK_1
channel ORA_AUX_DISK_1: SID=35 device type=DISK

channel ORA_AUX_DISK_1: starting datafile backup set restore
channel ORA_AUX_DISK_1: restoring control file
channel ORA_AUX_DISK_1: reading from backup piece
/u01/app/oracle/fast_recovery_area/ANITASDB/ANITASDB/autobackup/2017_06_22/o1_mf_s_94735
5211_dnrmrxbb_.bkp
channel ORA_AUX_DISK_1: piece
handle=/u01/app/oracle/fast_recovery_area/ANITASDB/ANITASDB/autobackup/2017_06_22/o1_mf_
s_947355211_dnrmrxbb_.bkp tag=TAG20170622T181331
channel ORA_AUX_DISK_1: restored backup piece 1
channel ORA_AUX_DISK_1: restore complete, elapsed time: 00:00:04
output file
name=/u01/app/oracle/fast_recovery_area/ANITASDB/ANITASDB/controlfile/o1_mf_dpbrzx1q_.ct
l
Finished restore at 11-JUL-17
```

```
sql statement: alter database mount clone database

contents of Memory Script:
{
# set requested point in time
set until scn 10952577;
# switch to valid datafilecopies
switch clone datafile 46 to datafilecopy

"/u01/app/oracle/oradata/JOHNSPDB2/ANITASDB/4F20CED2900D14D4E055000000000001/datafile/o1
_mf_system_dlcz6om3_.dbf";
switch clone datafile 47 to datafilecopy

"/u01/app/oracle/oradata/JOHNSPDB2/ANITASDB/4F20CED2900D14D4E055000000000001/datafile/o1
_mf_sysaux_dlcz6omj_.dbf";
switch clone datafile 48 to datafilecopy

"/u01/app/oracle/oradata/JOHNSPDB2/ANITASDB/4F20CED2900D14D4E055000000000001/datafile/o1
_mf_undotbs1_dlcz6omk_.dbf";
switch clone datafile 49 to datafilecopy

"/u01/app/oracle/oradata/ANITASDB/4F20CED2900D14D4E055000000000001/datafile/o1_mf_users_
dpbp6c79_.dbf";
# set destinations for recovery set and auxiliary set datafiles
set newname for datafile 1 to

"/u01/app/oracle/fast_recovery_area/ANITASDB/ANITASDB/datafile/o1_mf_system_dpbs1409_.db
f";
set newname for datafile 4 to

"/u01/app/oracle/fast_recovery_area/ANITASDB/ANITASDB/datafile/o1_mf_undotbs1_dpbs14nn_.
dbf";
set newname for datafile 3 to

"/u01/app/oracle/fast_recovery_area/ANITASDB/ANITASDB/datafile/o1_mf_sysaux_dpbs14o5_.db
f";
set newname for datafile 7 to

"/u01/app/oracle/fast_recovery_area/ANITASDB/ANITASDB/datafile/o1_mf_users_dpbs1xjh_.dbf
";
# restore the tablespaces in the recovery set and the auxiliary set
restore clone datafile 1, 4, 3, 7;

switch clone datafile all;
}
executing Memory Script

executing command: SET until clause

datafile 46 switched to datafile copy
input datafile copy RECID=4 STAMP=949085422 file
name=/u01/app/oracle/oradata/JOHNSPDB2/ANITASDB/4F20CED2900D14D4E055000000000001/datafil
e/o1_mf_system_dlcz6om3_.dbf

datafile 47 switched to datafile copy
input datafile copy RECID=5 STAMP=949085422 file
name=/u01/app/oracle/oradata/JOHNSPDB2/ANITASDB/4F20CED2900D14D4E055000000000001/datafil
e/o1_mf_sysaux_dlcz6omj_.dbf

datafile 48 switched to datafile copy
input datafile copy RECID=6 STAMP=949085422 file
name=/u01/app/oracle/oradata/JOHNSPDB2/ANITASDB/4F20CED2900D14D4E055000000000001/datafil
e/o1_mf_undotbs1_dlcz6omk_.dbf

datafile 49 switched to datafile copy
input datafile copy RECID=7 STAMP=949085422 file
name=/u01/app/oracle/oradata/ANITASDB/4F20CED2900D14D4E055000000000001/datafile/o1_mf_us
ers_dpbp6c79_.dbf

executing command: SET NEWNAME

executing command: SET NEWNAME

executing command: SET NEWNAME

executing command: SET NEWNAME

Starting restore at 11-JUL-17
using channel ORA_AUX_DISK_1


Removing automatic instance
```

```
shutting down automatic instance
Oracle instance shut down
Automatic instance removed
auxiliary instance file /
```

Recover a Dropped Pluggable Database

If you issued the **DROP PLUGGABLE DATABASE** command, you cannot reuse a previously taken backup of this particular PDB anymore to recover the PDB into the existing CDB. To restore, we need to follow these steps:

- Recover the backup including this particular PDB to an auxiliary CDB.
- Unplug the dropped PDB after recovery has been finished and plug it back into the original CDB.

Please review the My Oracle Support document #2034953.1: *How to Restore - Dropped Pluggable database (PDB) in Multitenant* which describes the step-by-step workflow.

Flashing Back a Single PDB

Use Case: Our team's QA manager wants to run several application workload tests against the QA_HR PDB on CDB2. The objective is to make sure that the database is reset to its initial state, before restarting a new test series. We'll therefore leverage a new 12.2 feature, **FLASHBACK PLUGGABLE DATABASE**, to rewind the QA_HR PDB to its initial "golden" state after each test is completed and before the next round of QA testing starts.

On CDB2, let's enable **FLASHBACK DATABASE** operations for that container database.

```
SQL@CDB2> ALTER SESSION SET CONTAINER = CDB$ROOT;
Session altered.

SQL@CDB2> ALTER DATABASE FLASHBACK ON;
Database altered.
```

Note that the change of state for **CDB2** is reflected in CDB2's alert log as well.

```
. . .
alter database flashback on
Starting background process RVWR
2017-06-20T12:49:53.554235-05:00
RVWR started with pid=26, OS id=13138
2017-06-20T12:49:59.327469-05:00
Allocated 15937344 bytes in shared pool for flashback generation buffer
2017-06-20T12:50:05.885871-05:00
Flashback Database Enabled at SCN 5469926
Completed: alter database flashback on
. . .
```

Next, we'll create a guaranteed restore point named GOLDEN for this PDB's current state, before we apply any DML to QA_HR.

```
SQL@CDB2> ALTER SESSION SET CONTAINER = QA_HR;
Session altered.

SQL@CDB2> CREATE RESTORE POINT golden
               FOR PLUGGABLE DATABASE qa_hr
               GUARANTEE FLASHBACK DATABASE;
Restore point created.
```

To confirm the details of the restore point we've just created, we can execute the SQL statements in verify_PDB_RestorePoints.sql.

```
/*
|| Script:  Verify_PDB_RestorePoints.sql
|| Purpose: Lists all current PDB-level restore points and their
attributes
*/

SET LINESIZE 120
SET PAGESIZE 2000
COL pdb_name               FORMAT A12        HEADING "PDB Name"
COL rp_name                FORMAT A08        HEADING
"Restore|Point|Name"
COL scn                    FORMAT 9999999    HEADING "SCN"
COL database_incarnation#  FORMAT 9999       HEADING "DB|Inc|#"
COL pdb_incarnation#       FORMAT 9999       HEADING "PDB|Inc|#"
COL preserved              FORMAT A06        HEADING "Pres-|erved?"
COL clean_rp               FORMAT A08        HEADING "Clean|RP?"
COL gfdb_ind               FORMAT A06        HEADING
"Guar|Flash|Back|DB?"
COL storage_mb             FORMAT 999999     HEADING
"Space|Used|(MB)"
COL time_dtm               FORMAT A19        HEADING "Timestamp"
COL rp_dtm                 FORMAT A19        HEADING "RP Timestamp"

TTITLE "PDB Restore Points|(from V$RESTORE_POINT)"
SELECT
     P.name pdb_name
    ,RP.name rp_name
    ,scn
    ,database_incarnation#
    ,pdb_incarnation#
    ,preserved
    ,clean_pdb_restore_point clean_rp
    ,guarantee_flashback_database gfdb_ind
    ,(storage_size /(1024*1024)) storage_mb
    ,TO_CHAR(time, 'YYYY-MM-DD.HH24:MI') act_dtm
    ,TO_CHAR(restore_point_time, 'YYYY-MM-DD.HH24:MI') rp_dtm
  FROM
     v$restore_point RP
    ,v$pdbs p
 WHERE P.con_id = RP.con_id
```

```
  AND RP.pdb_restore_point <> 'NO'
;
TTITLE OFF

SET LINESIZE 80
SET PAGESIZE 2000
COL pdb_name                   FORMAT A12        HEADING "PDB Name"
COL incarnation_scn            FORMAT 9999999    HEADING "Incar-
|Nation|SCN"
COL db_incarnation#            FORMAT 999999     HEADING "CDB|Incar-
|Nation|#"
COL pdb_incarnation#           FORMAT 999999     HEADING "PDB|Incar-
|Nation|#"
COL fda_ind                    FORMAT A06        HEADING
"Flash|Back|DB|Alwd?"
COL incarnation_dtm            FORMAT A19        HEADING "Timestamp"
COL status                     FORMAT A08        HEADING "Status"

TTITLE "PDB Incarnations|(from V$PDB_INCARNATION)"
SELECT
      P.name pdb_name
     ,incarnation_scn
     ,db_incarnation#
     ,pdb_incarnation#
     ,TO_CHAR(incarnation_time, 'YYYY-MM-DD.HH24:MI') incarnation_dtm
     ,status
     ,flashback_database_allowed fda_ind
  FROM
      v$pdb_incarnation PI
     ,v$pdbs P
  WHERE P.con_id = PI.con_id
  ORDER BY P.name, PI.pdb_incarnation#
;
TTITLE OFF
```

```
SQL@CDB2> @Verify_PDB_RestorePoints.sql
                              PDB Restore Points
                             (from V$RESTORE_POINT)

                                              Guar
         Restore        DB   PDB              Flash  Space
PDB      Point          Inc  Inc Pres- Clean  Back   Used
Name     Name      SCN  #    #   erved? RP?   DB?    (MB) ACT_DTM          RP Timestamp
-------- -------- ----- ---- --- ------ ----- ----- ----- ---------------- ------------------
QA_HR    GOLDEN  5470455  2    0 YES    NO    YES    200 2017-06-20.12:59

                              PDB Incarnations
                            (from V$PDB_INCARNATION)

                      CDB     PDB                              Flash
              Incar-  Incar-  Incar-                           Back
              Nation  Nation  Nation                           DB
PDB Name      SCN     #       # Timestamp           Status     Alwd?
-------- ----------- ------- --- ----------------   --------   -----
QA_HR             1       1    0 2017-01-26.13:52   PARENT     YES
QA_HR       1408558       2    0 2017-05-19.16:13   CURRENT    YES
```

Now, let's capture the current state of QA_HR before we apply any additional transactions against it.

```
SQL@CDB2> @Verify_HR_DML.sql
```

LAST_NAME	SALARY	COMMISSION_PCT
Austin	4800	
Ernst	6000	
Hunold	9000	
Lorentz	4200	
Pataballa	4800	

To demonstrate the success of the PDB-level FLASHBACK DATABASE operation, we'll generate some additional transactions against the HR.EMPLOYEES table in QA_HR.

```
SQL@CDB2> @Generate_HR_DML.sql
5 rows updated.
Commit complete.

SQL@CDB2> @Verify_HR_DML.sql
```

LAST_NAME	SALARY	COMMISSION_PCT
Austin	96783.22	.21
Ernst	78634.83	.07
Hunold	73424.06	.09
Lorentz	110637.43	.16
Pataballa	2677.67	.02

Now, let's flash back the QA_HR PDB to a previous incarnation. Note: don't forget to execute these commands from within the PDB itself.

```
SQL@CDB2> ALTER PLUGGABLE DATABASE qa_hr CLOSE;
Pluggable database altered.

SQL@CDB2> FLASHBACK PLUGGABLE DATABASE qa_hr TO RESTORE POINT golden;
Flashback complete.

SQL@CDB2> ALTER PLUGGABLE DATABASE OPEN RESETLOGS;
Pluggable database altered.
```

For confirmation, here are the results of these commands from the perspective of CDB2's alert log.

```
. . .
QA_HR(4):alter pluggable database close
2017-06-20T13:19:59.660148-05:00
QA_HR(4):JIT: pid 14164 requesting stop
2017-06-20T13:20:04.285918-05:00
Pluggable database QA_HR closed
QA_HR(4):Completed: alter pluggable database close
2017-06-20T13:20:44.047448-05:00
QA_HR(4):flashback pluggable database to restore point golden
2017-06-20T13:20:45.540672-05:00
QA_HR(4):Flashback Restore Start
2017-06-20T13:20:48.808889-05:00
QA_HR(4):Restore Flashback Pluggable Database QA_HR (4) until change
5470456
QA_HR(4):Flashback Restore Complete
QA_HR(4):Flashback Media Recovery Start
2017-06-20T13:20:49.150233-05:00
QA_HR(4):Serial Media Recovery started
2017-06-20T13:20:50.809603-05:00
QA_HR(4):Recovery of Online Redo Log: Thread 1 Group 3 Seq 27 Reading
mem 0
QA_HR(4):   Mem# 0: +DATA/CDB2/ONLINELOG/group_3.295.944410409
QA_HR(4):   Mem# 1: +RECO/CDB2/ONLINELOG/group_3.267.944410629
2017-06-20T13:20:51.280653-05:00
QA_HR(4):Incomplete Recovery applied until change 5470456 time
06/20/2017 12:59:40
QA_HR(4):Flashback Media Recovery Complete
QA_HR(4):Flashback Pluggable Database QA_HR (4) recovered until change
5470456
```

```
QA_HR(4):Completed: flashback pluggable database to restore point
golden
2017-06-20T13:21:07.225338-05:00
QA_HR(4):alter pluggable database open resetlogs
2017-06-20T13:21:08.620729-05:00
Online datafile 38
Online datafile 37
Online datafile 36
Online datafile 35
Online datafile 34
Online datafile 33
2017-06-20T13:21:10.470208-05:00
QA_HR(4):Autotune of undo retention is turned on.
2017-06-20T13:21:10.818706-05:00
QA_HR(4):Endian type of dictionary set to little
2017-06-20T13:21:14.345449-05:00
QA_HR(4):[14164] Successfully onlined Undo Tablespace 2.
. .
QA_HR(4):Opening pdb with no Resource Manager plan active
2017-06-20T13:21:41.310202-05:00
Starting control autobackup

2017-06-20T13:21:53.814647-05:00
Control autobackup written to DISK device

handle '+RECO/CDB2/AUTOBACKUP/2017_06_20/s_947164901.279.947164911'

Pluggable database QA_HR closed
QA_HR(4):Completed: alter pluggable database open resetlogs
. . .
```

To confirm that we have flashed back the **QA_HR** database successfully to its prior restore point and prior incarnation via the queries use script **Verify_PDB_RestorePoints.sql**.

```
SQL@CDB2> @Verify_PDB_RestorePoints.sql
                            PDB Restore Points
                          (from V$RESTORE_POINT)

                                        Guar
                                        Flash  Space
        Restore        DB   PDB         Back   Used
PDB     Point          Inc  Inc  Pres-  Clean  Back  Used
Name    Name     SCN   #    #    erved? RP?    DB?   (MB)  ACT_DTM              RP Timestamp
-----   -------  ----- ---  ---  -----  -----  ----  ----  -------------------  ------------------
QA_HR   GOLDEN   5470455  2   0   YES    NO     YES   200   2017-06-20.12:59

                            PDB Incarnations
                          (from V$PDB_INCARNATION)

                         CDB      PDB                                     Flash
                Incar-   Incar-   Incar-                                  Back
                Nation   Nation   Nation                                  DB
PDB Name        SCN      #        # Timestamp              Status         Alwd?
--------------  -------  -------  ---------------------     -------------  -----
QA_HR           1408558  2        0 2017-05-19.16:13        PARENT         YES
QA_HR           5470456  2        1 2017-06-20.12:59        CURRENT        YES
```

Finally, let's verify that the original state of **QA_HR** as of the **GOLDEN** restore point has been restored.

```
SQL@CDB2> @Verify_HR_DML.sql

LAST_NAME                    SALARY COMMISSION_PCT
--------------------------   ------ --------------
Austin                         4800
Ernst                          6000
Hunold                         9000
Lorentz                        4200
Pataballa                      4800
```

Note: even though the QA_HR PDB has progressed to a new incarnation, it's at the same SCN it was before the ALTER DATABASE OPEN RESETLOGS; operation, and the initial state of table HR.EMPLOYEES has been successfully restored.

8. Winning Performance Challenging in Oracle Multitenant

Introduction to this Chapter

Oracle Multitenant option has introduced a fresh and intuitive approach for implementing database consolidation, and at the same time, it has provided an easy solution to address some of the key database consolidation challenges that companies dealt with in the pre-Oracle 12c era.

Using the Oracle Multitenant option for database consolidation is great, as it can reduce costs for companies, and make DBAs more efficient - by allowing them to manage many (pluggable) databases as one. However, with "great power comes great responsibility", consolidating databases require ensuing that application performance SLAs won't be degraded as a result of the consolidation.
In this chapter, some key topics related to performance challenges when implementing database consolidation using Oracle Multitenant will be addressed in two sections:

- Ensuring high quality of service
- Performance Monitoring when using Oracle Multitenant

Ensuring High Quality of Service (QoS)

Whether you are running your Oracle Multitenant environments on premise or in the cloud, consolidating application pluggable databases into a single container database (CDB) will introduce a new quality of service challenge as many pluggable databases will compete over the same CDB resources. It is crucial to ensure a high-level quality of service for each application, so that it won't be too affected by the other pluggable databases workload.

Let's explore two simple examples:
1. An ERP application that has an inconsistent performance because, during the morning other pluggable databases on the same CDB are idle, but during evening time, other pluggable databases on the same CDB are very loaded - in other words, the PDBs are competing for system resources at various times.
2. HR application consumes too many resources, which could potentially impact other pluggable databases stability and performance.

As a DBA, you should strive to ensure consistent performance SLAs for the applications. There are various methods to ensure a high-level quality of service by setting the amount of resources each pluggable database may consume.

Oracle 12c Release 1

With the introduction of Oracle Multitenant in Oracle 12c Release 1, Oracle has enhanced the Oracle Resource Manager feature to support the Multitenant option, by setting **CPU Shares** for the pluggable databases. CPU Shares represent the proportion of the minimum guaranteed CPU resources for each pluggable database. In addition, Oracle allows setting a maximum CPU Utilization limit for each pluggable database.

By default, each PDB gets a single CPU share with no CPU utilization limit (CPU utilization limit = 100%). These defaults essentially mean that each PDB has the same priority (same minimum guaranteed CPU resources) and has no maximum CPU limits. In most cases, you would want to consider changing these default settings, because in the real world, some applications have higher priority compared to other applications. The defaults can be obtained by running the following queries:

```
SQL> SELECT plan_id,
            plan,
            comments,
            mandatory
    FROM dba_cdb_rsrc_plans
    WHERE plan = 'DEFAULT_CDB_PLAN';
```

PLAN_ID	PLAN	COMMENTS	MANDATORY
17349	DEFAULT_CDB_PLAN	Default CDB plan	YES

```
SQL> SELECT SHARES, UTILIZATION_LIMIT, PARALLEL_SERVER_LIMIT
    FROM DBA_CDB_RSRC_PLAN_DIRECTIVES
    WHERE  PLAN = 'DEFAULT_CDB_PLAN'
           AND PLUGGABLE_DATABASE = 'ORA$DEFAULT_PDB_DIRECTIVE';
```

SHARES	UTILIZATION_LIMIT	PARALLEL_SERVER_LIMIT
1	100	100

Let's assume we have the following 2 applications with the following settings:

- **OLTP** which has a minimum of 75% guaranteed CPU (3 out of 4 shares) and no maximum CPU limit (could potentially consume all CDB available CPU resources).
- **DWH** which has a minimum of 25% guaranteed CPU (1 out of 4 shares) and 60% maximum CPU limit out of the total available CDB CPU resources.

Pluggable Database	CPU Shares	Guaranteed CPU	CPU Limit
OLTP	3	3/4 = 75%	100%
DWH	1	1/4 = 25%	60%

Creating a Resource Manager Plan that enforces these settings can be done easily. For example, let's say we would like to create a resource manager plan that runs during daytime, we can create it as follows:

```
DECLARE
    daytime_plan VARCHAR2(30) := 'DAYTIME_CDB_PLAN';
BEGIN
    DBMS_RESOURCE_MANAGER.clear_pending_area;
    DBMS_RESOURCE_MANAGER.create_pending_area;

    DBMS_RESOURCE_MANAGER.create_cdb_plan(
    plan    => daytime_plan,
    comment => 'A daytime CDB resource plan');
    DBMS_RESOURCE_MANAGER.create_cdb_plan_directive(
    plan                  => daytime_plan,
    pluggable_database    => 'OLTP',
    shares                => 3,
    utilization_limit     => 100,
    parallel_server_limit => 100);

    DBMS_RESOURCE_MANAGER.create_cdb_plan_directive(
    plan                  => daytime_plan,
    pluggable_database    => 'DWH',
    shares                => 1,
    utilization_limit     => 60,
    parallel_server_limit => 100);

    DBMS_RESOURCE_MANAGER.validate_pending_area;
    DBMS_RESOURCE_MANAGER.submit_pending_area;
END;
/
```

Once we've created this resource manager plan, we can automate its schedule by creating a new time window using the Oracle Scheduler feature. The following example creates a window which defines that the "DAYTIME_CDB_PLAN" resource plan will be active every day starting from 08:00am PST time zone.

```
BEGIN
DBMS_SCHEDULER.CREATE_WINDOW (
    window_name        => 'DAYTIME_WINDOW',
    resource_plan      => 'DAYTIME_CDB_PLAN',
    start_date         => '15-JUL-03 8.00.00AM US/Pacific',
    repeat_interval    => 'FREQ=DAILY',
    duration           => interval '10' HOUR,
    comments           => 'Daytime window for CDB Resource Plan');
END;
/


SQL> SELECT START_DATE,
            REPEAT_INTERVAL,
            DURATION,
            ENABLED,
            ACTIVE
       FROM cdb_scheduler_windows
      WHERE window_name = 'DAYTIME_WINDOW';

START_DATE                      REPEAT_INTERVAL DURATION          ENABLED  ACTIVE
------------------------------- --------------- ----------------- -------- ------
15-JUL-03 08.00.00.00 AM US/PACIFIC  FREQ=DAILY  +000 10:00:00     TRUE     FALSE
```

Oracle 12c Release 2 and Above

One of the biggest challenges in Oracle 12c Release 1, was the inability to enforce memory and I/O resources to pluggable databases. The good news is that starting from 12c Release 2, this can be done easily by adjusting the following parameters at the PDB level:

Memory parameters
- **SGA_TARGET** - specifies the total size of all SGA components
- **DB_CACHE_SIZE** - specifies the size of the DEFAULT buffer pool for buffers with the primary block size
- **SHARED_POOL_SIZE** - specifies the size of the shared pool
- **PGA_AGGREGATE_LIMIT** - specifies a limit on the aggregate PGA memory consumed by the instance
- **PGA_AGGREGATE_TARGET** - specifies the target aggregate PGA memory available to all server processes attached to the instance
- **SGA_MIN_SIZE** - set minimum guaranteed SGA size for a PDB (new in 12c Release 2)

I/O parameters
- **MAX_IOPS** - limits number of I/O operations per second (new in 12c Release 2)
- **MAX_MBPS** - limits megabytes for I/O operations per second (new in 12c Release 2)

CPU parameters
- **CPU_COUNT** - specifies the number of CPUs available for the Database

Performance Monitoring when Using Oracle Multitenant

When using Oracle Multitenant, it is essential to monitor the entire CDB workload activity, as well as each pluggable database individual workload. By knowing how the workload is distributed across the various pluggable databases at different time frames; this will help Database Administrators to effectively choose the right approach for ensuring a high-level quality of service by using Oracle resource manager and the various parameters that have been described previously.
Once the CPU, Memory, and I/O resources have been set, the next step would be to validate that the workload is properly distributed according to the new settings.
In this section, it is time to explore several methods to monitor Oracle Multitenant environments:
- Dictionary Views
- Automatic Workload Repository (AWR)
- Monitoring Tools

Dictionary Views

In the previous section, we reviewed several new parameters which have been added since 12c release 2. These parameters can control CPU, memory, and I/O resource utilizations - at the pluggable database level.

When setting resource limitations, it's important to evaluate the historical ranges of CPU, Memory, and I/O metrics for each pluggable database, and based on that we could predict and expect future usage. An example of a useful dictionary view that could be used for that purpose is: **DBA_HIST_RSRC_PDB_METRIC**.

DBA_HIST_RSRC_PDB_METRIC displays information about the historical Resource Manager metrics for the past hour by PDB. Here is an example of a query that will help us determine the maximum values in the past hour for a specific PDB (with CON_ID = 3) for the following metrics: I/O operations per second, I/O megabytes per second, SGA usage, and PGA usage:

```
SQL> SELECT MAX(IOPS),
            MAX (IOMBPS),
            MAX (SGA_BYTES)/1024/1024 MAX_SGA_MB,
            MAX (PGA_BYTES)/1024/1024 MAX_PGB_MB
     FROM DBA_HIST_RSRC_PDB_METRIC
  WHERE CON_ID = 3  ;


MAX(IOPS)    MAX(IOMBPS)   MAX_SGA_MB   MAX_PGB_MB
----------   -----------   ----------   ----------
70.42618893  19.146447287  761.419693   56.08081532
```

Like all the other DBA_HIST_* views, the DBA_HIST_RSRC_PDB_METRIC relies on AWR tables. Looking only at the last hour might not be enough, and therefore it is possible to query the underlying AWR table (AWR_ROOT_RSRC_PDB_METRIC) in order to get more historical data.

AWR

AWR is another powerful method for monitoring and diagnosing workload and performance issues in multitenant environments. Starting with Oracle 12c Release 2, Oracle added the option to run AWR reports at the pluggable database level. Below is an example of how you could easily choose whether to run an AWR report at the container or at the specific pluggable database level:

```
SQL> @?/rdbms/admin/awrrpt.sql

Specify the Report Type
~~~~~~~~~~~~~~~~~~~~~~~~~
AWR reports can be generated in the following formats.  Please enter the
name of the format at the prompt.  Default value is 'html'.

'html'          HTML format (default)
'text'          Text format
'active-html'   Includes Performance Hub active report

Enter value for report_type: html
old   1: select 'Type Specified: ',lower(nvl('&&report_type','html')) report_type from dual
new   1: select 'Type Specified: ',lower(nvl('html','html')) report_type from dual

Type Specified: html

Specify the location of AWR Data   ◀━━━━
~~~~~~~~~~~~~~~~~~~~~~~~~~~~~~~~~~~~~
AWR_ROOT - Use AWR data from root (default)
AWR_PDB - Use AWR data from PDB
```

The expected output will be a regular AWR report at the CDB level and filtered at the pluggable database level (based on your selection).

Furthermore, starting from Oracle 12c Release 2, it is possible to manage AWR settings/operations at the PDB level (e.g. AWR data retention, snapshot schedule, taking manual snapshots, purging snapshot data).

Note that in 12cR2, Oracle has introduced a new parameter that affects AWR behavior in multitenant environments, **AWR_PDB_AUTOFLUSH_ENABLED**, which specifies whether to enable or disable AWR snapshots for all the pluggable database in a Container Database or for individual pluggable databases in a CDB. The reason it's important to be familiar with this parameter, is because the default value is "false", thus by default, automatic AWR snapshots are disabled for all the PDBs in a CDB. You might want to change that either at the CDB level, so that all pluggable databases in the CDB will have automatic AWR snapshots, or at the PDB level, for specific mission critical pluggable databases.

Monitoring Tools

When it comes to database monitoring and diagnostics, you can't fix what you can't see. Both dictionary views and AWR options could be helpful, but the lack of visualization makes it very challenging to effectively monitor Multitenant environments. Performance tuning is one of the most important DBA tasks, and while Oracle's Diagnostics pack can assist by providing access to Oracle Enterprise

Manager (OEM) Active Session History (ASH) Analytics, it is only available with OEM Enterprise Edition plus Diagnostics pack, which comes at a significant extra cost.

In other words, if you are not running your Oracle environments with the Diagnostics pack, Oracle tuning is probably challenging as AWRs and many useful dictionary views are simply not available. Instead, you're forced to fall back on legacy tools like Statspack, which requires rare expertise and makes the performance tuning process much longer and more complex.

What if you could simplify performance monitoring tuning in Oracle affordably? Turns out, you can get the powerful monitoring, diagnostics, and workload analysis you need to maintain peak Oracle performance, even without having Oracle Diagnostic and Tuning packs. With Quest® Foglight® for Oracle, you get 24x7 enterprise monitoring. This powerful analysis toolset supports all Oracle editions and configurations, at a much lower cost than Oracle's add-on packs.

In this section, you will see how Foglight can immediately boost the value of your existing Oracle databases while slashing your workload.

Foglight provides cross-database platform monitoring either on premise or in the cloud. It fully supports: Oracle, SQL Server, DB2, SAP Hana, SAP ASE, MongoDB, Cassandra, MySQL, PostgreSQL and Amazon RedShift.

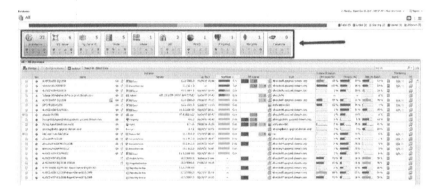

For Oracle Multitenant environments, Foglight has a dedicated "Pluggable Databases" dashboard that can display how the workload is distributed across the container database; furthermore, in case of Real Application Clusters (RAC), the dashboard displays for each PDB how its workload is distributed across all the RAC nodes.

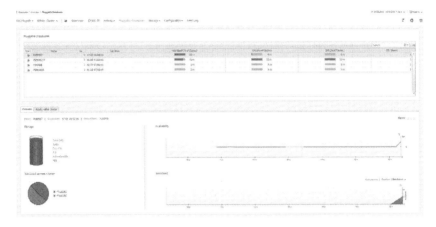

With that said, the true power of Foglight for Oracle comes with "Foglight Performance Investigator" analysis toolset. Let's look at just a few of the powerful performance diagnostics features in Foglight for Oracle.

Multi-Dimensional Analysis

The multi-dimensional analysis feature enables running Online Analytical Processing (OLAP) operations - such as drill-down, rollup, slice and dice on top of the database workload, including access to historical activity. This can be easily done by navigating in the performance tree at the left section of the screen, as follows:

For example, let's assume that we would like to see all the SQL statements and their associated performance statistics, which have been executed on pluggable database "PDBTEST" by user "SALES". This can be done, as follows:

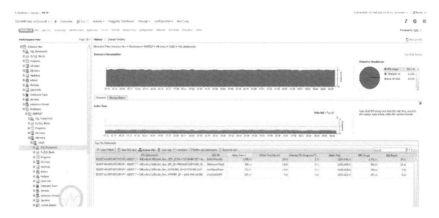

Another powerful capability with the multi-dimensional analysis is to analyze current and historical blocking locks in a very quick and intuitive manner. In the following screenshot, you can see all the blocking locks tree for an instance. This tree will display key information regarding the blocking lock events. For example, at what time the blocking lock event started, what was the duration of the lock, what is the text of the blocked SQL statements, and other useful details about the blocker and the blocked sessions (such as SID, user name, program, machine).

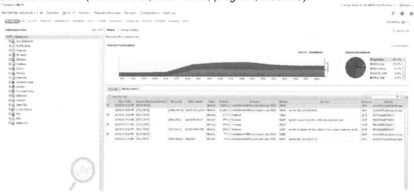

When using Multitenant, Foglight will allow you to slice all the blocking locks activity for a given pluggable database, as follows:

In the above screenshot, you can see that the locks tree is filtered by the "OLTP" pluggable database.

Baselining

Foglight baseline algorithm, IntelliProfile™, defines the expected behavior during different time periods (a given hour in a day, day in a week, week in a month and so on). It enables you to quickly understand whether database performance is stable and as expected, or, has deviated from the baseline.

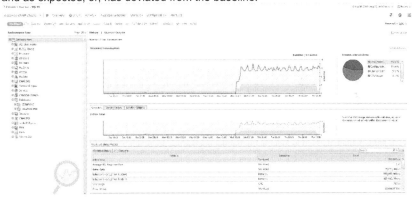

Compare

Foglight for Oracle supports both instance-level comparisons and dimension-level comparisons, so you can easily compare the performance of different users, SQL statements, pluggable databases, and more.

When implementing database consolidation using the Oracle Multitenant option, the compare feature could be extremely useful in case you are interested in comparing performance metrics and want to visualize the differences in the workload between two different pluggable databases.

Change Tracking

Foglight for Oracle displays schema changes, execution plan changes, Oracle configuration changes, and operating system (OS) changes in one consolidated chart; providing you with a unique solution for correlating the changes with database workload. Like all the other features in Foglight for Oracle, change tracking also fully supports Multitenant environments.

Chapter Summary

Database consolidation can reduce costs and make database administration easier and more efficient by allowing DBAs to manage many (pluggable) databases as one and spend less time on the repetitive administrative tasks. This enables DBAs to spend more time on innovation and focus on bringing more value to the business.

However, with great power comes great responsibility. When many pluggable databases are consolidated into a single container database, they will compete over the same resources; therefore, it's crucial to know the right methods that will help you ensure a high level quality of service for your applications.

Managing Oracle Multitenant environments and ensuring high level of quality of service could be very challenging, especially, when not having the right tools. With Foglight for Oracle, you can proactively monitor your Oracle databases and Multitenant environments without breaking the bank on Oracle Diagnostics packs. As we've seen, Foglight for Oracle provides a range of extremely powerful performance diagnostic features that will help you be more efficient and effective at ensuring peak database performance.

Ready to learn more? Visit quest.com/ products/foglight-for-oracle to take a product tour, read about how Foglight for Oracle has helped organizations like yours, or start your free trial today.

9. Resource Control and Governance

Limiting application developers and junior DBAs from executing commands, or using privileges that we've deemed inappropriate, within the confines of a development PDB is an important measure to take. We'll create a PDB Lockdown Profile that will prevent inadvertent and/or dangerous changes to some initialization parameters, while allowing others to be executed.

First, let's connect to CDB1, and then create a PDB Lockdown Profile that will limit any user in a PDB from using privileges and commands that are deemed inaccessible. Script `CreateLockdownProfile.sql` first creates a PDB Lockdown Profile named **NOTADBA**, and then alters that Lockdown Profile to prohibit changes to most initialization parameters. It also forbids the capability to create a partitioned object, for any user within a PDB that's assigned this Lockdown Profile. The script also shows the results of creating the Lockdown Profile as recorded in **DBA_LOCKDOWN_PROFILES**.

```
/*
|| Script:  Create_PDBLockdownProfile.sql
|| Purpose: Constructs a PDB Lockdown Profile named NOTADBA
||
*/


-----
-- Build PDB Lockdown Profile
-----

CREATE LOCKDOWN PROFILE notadba;

ALTER LOCKDOWN PROFILE notadba
    DISABLE STATEMENT = ('ALTER SYSTEM')
             CLAUSE = ('SET')
    OPTION ALL EXCEPT = ('PLSQL_CODE_TYPE'
                        ,'PLSQL_DEBUG'
                        ,'PLSQL_WARNINGS'
                        );

ALTER LOCKDOWN PROFILE notadba
    DISABLE OPTION = ('PARTITIONING');

/*
-- Prohibited! (for now - only clause allowed is SET)
ALTER LOCKDOWN PROFILE notadba
    DISABLE STATEMENT = ('ALTER SYSTEM')
             CLAUSE = ('FLUSH')
    OPTION ALL EXCEPT = ('SHARED_POOL');
*/


-----
-- Verify Lockdown Profile attributes
-----
SET PAGESIZE 2000
SET LINESIZE 132
COL profile_name    FORMAT A16   HEADING "Profile Name"
COL rule_type       FORMAT A12   HEADING "Rule Type"
COL rule            FORMAT A24   HEADING "Rule"
COL status          FORMAT A08   HEADING "Status"
COL clause          FORMAT A08   HEADING "Clause"
COL clause_option   FORMAT A24   HEADING "Option"
COL option_value    FORMAT A12   HEADING "Option|Value"
```

```
COL min_value          FORMAT A08   HEADING "Minimum|Value"
COL max_value          FORMAT A08   HEADING "Maximum|Value"
COL list               FORMAT A08   HEADING "List"
TTITLE "PDB Lockdown Profiles|(from DBA_LOCKDOWN_PROFILES)"
SELECT
      profile_name
     ,rule_type
     ,rule
     ,status
     ,clause
     ,clause_option
     ,option_value
--   ,min_value
--   ,max_value
--   ,list
  FROM dba_lockdown_profiles
 ORDER BY profile_name, rule_type, rule, status
;
TTITLE OFF
```

```
$> . oraenv
ORACLE_SID = [oracle] ? CDB1
The Oracle base remains unchanged with value /u01/app/oracle

$> sqlplus / as sysdba
SQL*Plus: Release 12.2.0.1.0 Production on Thu Jun 15 19:07:44 2017
Copyright (c) 1982, 2016, Oracle.  All rights reserved.
Connected to:
Oracle Database 12c Enterprise Edition Release 12.2.0.1.0 - 64bit
Production

SQL@CDB1> @Create_PDBLockdownProfile.sql

Lockdown Profile created.

Lockdown Profile altered.

Lockdown Profile altered.

PDB Lockdown Profiles
(from DBA_LOCKDOWN_PROFILES)
```

Profile Name	Rule Type	Rule	Status	Clause	Option Value
NOTADBA	OPTION	PARTITIONING	DISABLE		
NOTADBA	STATEMENT	ALTER SYSTEM	DISABLE	SET	
NOTADBA	STATEMENT	ALTER SYSTEM	ENABLE	SET	PLSQL_DEBUG
NOTADBA	STATEMENT	ALTER SYSTEM	ENABLE	SET	PLSQL_CODE_TYPE
NOTADBA	STATEMENT	ALTER SYSTEM	ENABLE	SET	PLSQL_WARNINGS
PRIVATE_DBAAS			EMPTY		
PUBLIC_DBAAS			EMPTY		
SAAS			EMPTY		

To apply this PDB Lockdown Profile to the **DEV_HR** PDB, connect to it and then alter the **PDB_LOCKDOWN** initialization parameter.

```
SQL@CDB1> ALTER SESSION SET CONTAINER = DEV_HR;
Session altered.

SQL@CDB1> ALTER SYSTEM SET pdb_lockdown = NOTADBA;
System altered.

SQL@CDB1> SHOW PARAMETER pdb
```

```
NAME                                  TYPE                          VALUE
------------------------------------  ----------------------------  ----------------
----------
autotask_max_active_pdbs              integer                       2
awr_pdb_autoflush_enabled             boolean                       FALSE
disable_pdb_feature                   big integer                   0
enable_automatic_maintenance_pdb      boolean                       TRUE
enabled_PDBs_on_standby               string                        *
max_datapump_jobs_per_pdb             integer                       100
max_pdbs                              integer                       4098
one_step_plugin_for_pdb_with_tde      boolean                       FALSE
ndb_file_name_convert                 string
pdb_lockdown                          string                        NOTADBA
pdb_os_credential                     string
target_pdbs                           integer                       8
```

Connect to DEV_HR as the SYSTEM user account, and then open script
Test_PDBLockdownProfile.sql to cut and paste the following commands into your
terminal session to see what happens. This procedure will let us see what users of
the DEV_HR PDB can and cannot do!

```
/*
|| Script:  Test_PDBLockdownProfile.sql
|| Purpose: Tests PDB Lockdown Profile NOTADBA for a specific PDB
(DEV_AP)
*/

CONNECT sys/oracle_4U@dev_ap AS SYSDBA;

-- Should succeed!
ALTER SYSTEM SET plsql_debug = TRUE;

-- Should succeed!
ALTER SYSTEM FLUSH BUFFER_CACHE;

-- Should fail!
ALTER SYSTEM SET cursor_sharing = FORCE;

-- Should fail!
ALTER SYSTEM SET pdb_lockdown = '';
```

You'll note similar results to these.

```
SQL@CDB1> CONNECT system/oracle_4U@dev_hr
Connected.

SQL@CDB1> ALTER SYSTEM SET plsql_debug = TRUE;
System altered.

SQL@CDB1> ALTER SYSTEM FLUSH BUFFER_CACHE;
System altered.

SQL@CDB1> ALTER SYSTEM SET cursor_sharing = FORCE;
alter system set cursor_sharing=force
*
ERROR at line 1:
ORA-01031: insufficient privileges

SQL@CDB1> alter system set sga_max_size=2048M scope=spfile;
alter system set sga_max_size=2048M scope=spfile
*
ERROR at line 1:
```

One more test – can we create a partitioned table? Let's try with the commands in script `Create_PartitionedTable.sql`.

```
/*
 | Script:  Create_PartitionedTable.sql
 | Purpose: Attempts to create a partitioned table to prove out the NOTDBA
 |          PDB Lockdown Profile. (It should fail!)
*/

DROP TABLE hr.employee_invoices PURGE;
CREATE TABLE hr.employee_invoices (
    invoice_id  NUMBER(12)
    ,item_id NUMBER(9)
    ,sales_amt NUMBER(12,2)
    ,wholesale_cost  NUMBER(12,2)
)
    PARTITION BY HASH (invoice_id)
    PARTITIONS 4
    STORE IN (AP_DATA)
;
```

```
SQL@CDB1> @Create_PartitionedTable.sql;

SQL> 2  3  4  5  6  7  8  9  10 CREATE TABLE hr.employee_invoices (
*
ERROR at line 1:
ORA-00439: feature not enabled: Partitioning
```

To clean up before the next lab, let's drop the **NOTADBA** PDB Lockdown Profile at the CDB level on CDB1.

```
SQL@CDB1> exit;
$> sqlplus / as sysdba
. . .

SQL@CDB1> DROP LOCKDOWN PROFILE notadba;

SQL > Lockdown profile dropped.
```

Implementing PDB Resource Governance

The most common use case for implementing pluggable database environments is to create a high consolidation platform to migrate any kind of database and consolidate them onto container databases. As we increase our consolidation density and address different workloads on databases, we face the challenge of "noisy neighbors" where other databases can impact performance of neighboring databases. In Oracle 12.2, we have the capability to limit the I/O, CPU, and memory resources of each PDB to help eliminate potential noisy neighbors.

Here are some facts for you to consider as you set disk I/O resource management:
1. These parameters are only applicable for the multi-tenant option and they are not available for the Exadata engineered systems.
2. Oracle will not block what it considers to be critical I/O such as control file writes, password file I/O or DBWR IO writes. These writes will still be considered as part of accounting for the throttling algorithms. You may set one of the parameters or both of the parameters: MAX_IOPS and MAX_MBPS.
3. If the parameters are set at the CDB level, it becomes the default values for all PDBs. As they are set at the PDB level, the PDB settings override the default values set at the CDB level.
4. Setting very low value for IOPs is not recommended. For example, setting MAX_IOPS to 100 should not be considered. If you are governing I/O and if Oracle is limiting IO in various capacities, you will notice a resource manager wait event called resmgr: I/O rate limit.

In the previous release, we were able to instance cage a database by specifying the amount of CPU to a database. In Oracle 12.2, we can instance cage a CPU at the PDB level.

Please leverage this parameter carefully and properly architect the amount of CPU assigned at the PDB level. Oracle does allow over provisioning, which if not used correctly can get you in trouble. In the production environment, we do not encourage overprovisioning of memory or CPU. In the lower environments, we recommend that you over provision to see the ROI in your investments.

First, connect to the DEV_HR PDB database. We have provided a simple script called conn.sql to easily connect to a PDB.

```
@conn dev_hr
```

Once connected to the DEV_HR PDB, execute the `set_cpu_count.sql` script to set the CPU_COUNT for this instance to 1.

```
Filename: set_cpu_count.sql
alter system set cpu_count=1 scope=both
/
```

Execute the script called **pdb_params.sql** to view the modified parameters for the PDB. You will notice that the cpu_count parameter is set to 1.

Limiting IO On the CDB (Throttling Across Every PDB)

Now, we want to throttle the I/O for one or more PDBs, or for all PDBs, within a specific CDB. From the root container, execute the `io_max.sql` script to set MAX_IOPS to 400 and throughput to 100MB per second. Setting I/O limits at the CDB level sets the default I/O limits for all the PDBs.

```
Filename: io_max.sql
-- CONN / AS SYSDBA

-- Set IOPs and Throughput for ALL PDBs
ALTER SYSTEM SET max_iops=400 SCOPE=BOTH;
ALTER SYSTEM SET max_mbps=100 SCOPE=BOTH;
```

To disable I/O throttling at the CDB level execute the `io_reset.sql` script.

```
Filename: io_reset.sql
-- Remove defaults.
ALTER SYSTEM SET max_iops=0 SCOPE=BOTH;
ALTER SYSTEM SET max_mbps=0 SCOPE=BOTH;
```

As you see, we simply set the values for MAX_IOPS and MAX_MPBS to zero to disable I/O limits.

Limiting I/O on a Specific PDB

Login to one or more PDBs and execute the following ALTER SYSTEM commands.

```
Filename: io_max.sql
-- Set IOPs and Throughput for ALL PDBs
ALTER SYSTEM SET max_iops=200 SCOPE=BOTH;
ALTER SYSTEM SET max_mbps=20 SCOPE=BOTH;
```

View the modified parameters by executing the **pdb_params.sql** script; this will display all the modified parameters for all the PDBs. This script excludes the parameters for the root container and the seed container (PDB$SEED).

```
Filename: pdb_params.sql
col name for a55
col value for a55
set lines 255 trims on
SELECT con_id, NAME, value , isdefault, ismodified
FROM V$SYSTEM_PARAMETER
WHERE ISPDB_MODIFIABLE='TRUE'
and con_id not in (0,2)
```

```
ORDER BY con_id, ismodified, NAME;
```

This output is only for the **DEV_HR** PDB. If you connect to the root container and execute the same script, you will see PDB specific parameters for ALL the PDBs. Here is what the sample output should look like for the relevant PDB specific parameters.

```
SQL> @pdb_params
```

CON_ID	PDB_NAME	NAME	VALUE	ISDEFAULT	ISMODIFI
5	DEV_HR	common_user_prefix		TRUE	FALSE	
5	DEV_HR	db_cache_size	0	TRUE	FALSE
5	DEV_HR	optimizer_dynamic_sampling 2		TRUE	FALSE	
5	DEV_HR	optimizer_mode	ALL_ROWS	TRUE	FALSE
5	DEV_HR	query_rewrite_enabled	TRUE	TRUE	FALSE
5	DEV_HR	resource_manager_plan		TRUE	FALSE
5	DEV_HR	sga_target	0	FALSE	FALSE
5	DEV_HR	shared_pool_size	0	TRUE	FALSE
5	DEV_HR	skip_unusable_indexes	TRUE	TRUE	FALSE
5	DEV_HR	undo_tablespace	UNDOTBS1	FALSE	FALSE
5	DEV_HR	max_iops	200	TRUE	MODIFIED
5	DEV_HR	max_mbps	20	TRUE	MODIFIED

```
12 rows selected.
```

Notice the MAX_IOPS and MAX_MBPS parameters have been modified to the correct settings.

To disable IO throttling at the PDB level, execute the following script after connecting to the PDB.

```
Filename: io_reset.sql
-- Remove defaults.
ALTER SYSTEM SET max_iops=0 SCOPE=BOTH;
ALTER SYSTEM SET max_mbps=0 SCOPE=BOTH;
```

As you see, we simply set the values for MAX_IOPS and MAX_MPBS to zero to disable I/O limits.

Throttling Memory Limits for a PDB

Next, we are going to limit the **SGA_MIN_SIZE** to be 100M and set the **SGA_TARGET** to 200M for only the **DEV_HR** PDB. After connecting to the **DEV_HR** PDB database, execute the **set_cpu_limits.sql** script, to set the values for **SGA_MIN_SIZE** and **SGA_TARGET**.

```
$ cat set_sga_limits.sql
alter system set sga_min_size=100m scope=both;
alter system set SGA_TARGET=200m scope=both;
```

Execute the script called **pdb_params.sql** to view the modified parameters for the PDB. You will notice that the **SGA_MIN_SIZE** is set to 100M and **SGA_TARGET** is set to 200M.

Utilizing PDB-Level Heat Maps, Information Lifecycle Management (ILM), and Automatic Data Optimization (ADO)

Use Case: Our PROD_AP PDB is growing in size by leaps and bounds, but because we have limited flash storage resources, we must insure that only the "hottest" data is leveraging that storage. We'll build the infrastructure to compress data that's no longer being actively accessed by our application workloads, and then we'll implement a set of ILM ADO policies to automatically compress the data that's growing "colder." Once again, we'll test these new ILM ADO policies to insure they work as expected.

First, create a new partitioned table, AP.RANDOMIZED_PARTED, and load it with enough data to demonstrate how ILM ADO policies work. Note that some of the partitioned data in this table will reside in two tablespaces we've not yet used– ADO_COLD_DATA and ADO_COLD_IDX –. This is to demonstrate what happens to those partitions after ILM ADO policies are applied, when the data is no longer being actively accessed by application workloads.

The code in script Create_ADO_Objects.sql takes care of creating this new table.

```
/*
|| Script:  Create_ADO_Objects.sql
|| Purpose: Creates objects for ILM ADO demonstration
*/
DROP TABLE ap.randomized_parted PURGE;
CREATE TABLE ap.randomized_parted (
    key_id      NUMBER(8)
    ,key_date    DATE
    ,key_desc    VARCHAR2(32)
    ,key_sts     NUMBER(2) NOT NULL
)
PARTITION BY RANGE(key_date) (
    PARTITION P4_COLD
        VALUES LESS THAN (TO_DATE('2012-01-01','yyyy-mm-dd'))
        TABLESPACE ado_cold_data
    ,PARTITION P3_COOL
        VALUES LESS THAN (TO_DATE('2015-01-01','yyyy-mm-dd'))
        TABLESPACE ado_cold_data
    ,PARTITION P2_WARM
        VALUES LESS THAN (TO_DATE('2016-12-01','yyyy-mm-dd'))
        TABLESPACE ado_cold_data
    ,PARTITION P1_HOT
        VALUES LESS THAN (MAXVALUE)
        TABLESPACE ap_data NOCOMPRESS)
    NOLOGGING PARALLEL 4;

TRUNCATE TABLE ap.randomized_parted;

SET TIMING ON
SET SERVEROUTPUT ON
DECLARE
    ctr NUMBER := 0;
BEGIN
    FOR ctr IN 1..1000000
        LOOP
            INSERT INTO ap.randomized_parted
            VALUES(
                ctr
```

```
                 ,(TO_DATE('12/31/2016','mm/dd/yyyy') -
DBMS_RANDOM.VALUE(1,3650))
                 ,LPAD(' ',DBMS_RANDOM.VALUE(1,32),
SUBSTR('abcdefghijklmnopqrstuvwxyz',DBMS_RANDOM.VALUE(1,26), 1))
                 ,DECODE(MOD(ROUND(DBMS_RANDOM.VALUE(1,1000000),0),100)
                        , 0,30,  1,40,  2,40,  3,40,  4,40
                        , 5,20,  6,40,  7,40,  8,40,  9,30
                        ,10,40, 11,20, 12,10, 13,15, 14,30, 50)
               );
            IF MOD(ctr, 250000) = 0 THEN
               COMMIT;
            END IF;
        END LOOP;

        COMMIT;

EXCEPTION
    WHEN OTHERS THEN
    BEGIN
        DBMS_OUTPUT.PUT_LINE('Fatal exception while loading: ' ||
sqlcode || ' - ' || sqlerrm);
    END;
END;
/
SET TIMING OFF

ALTER TABLE ap.randomized_parted
    DROP CONSTRAINT randomized_parted_pk;

DROP INDEX ap.randomized_parted_pk;

ALTER TABLE ap.randomized_parted
    ADD CONSTRAINT randomized_parted_pk
    PRIMARY KEY (key_id)
    USING INDEX (
      CREATE UNIQUE INDEX ap.randomized_parted_pk
         ON ap.randomized_parted(key_id)
         TABLESPACE ado_cold_idx
         NOLOGGING
         PARALLEL 4
         );

BEGIN
    DBMS_STATS.GATHER_TABLE_STATS(
         ownname => 'AP'
         ,tabname => 'RANDOMIZED_PARTED'
         ,DEGREE => 4
         ,CASCADE => TRUE
    );
    DBMS_STATS.GATHER_TABLE_STATS(
         ownname => 'AP'
         ,tabname => 'RANDOMIZED_PARTED'
         ,method_opt => 'FOR ALL COLUMNS SIZE AUTO'
         ,CASCADE => TRUE
    );
    DBMS_STATS.GATHER_TABLE_STATS(
         ownname => 'AP'
         ,tabname => 'RANDOMIZED_PARTED'
         ,method_opt => 'FOR COLUMNS SIZE 10 key_sts'
         ,CASCADE => TRUE
    );
END;
/
```

```
SQL@CDB1> ALTER SESSION SET CONTAINER = PROD_AP;
Session altered.

SQL@CDB1> @Create_ADO_Objects.sql
Table dropped.
Table created.
Table truncated.
. . .
Commit complete.
Constraint created.
PL/SQL procedure complete.
```

We can review the current state of AP.RANDOMIZED_PARTED through the queries in Monitor_ADO_Objects.sql.

```
/*
|| Script:  Monitor_ADO_Objects.sql
|| Purpose: Shows current object statistics
*/

SET LINESIZE 130
SET PAGESIZE 2000

COL table_name       FORMAT A20 HEADING "Table"
COL tablespace_name  FORMAT A12 HEADING "Tablespace"
COL compression      FORMAT A12 HEADING "Compression|Level"
COL compress_for     FORMAT A40 HEADING "Compress|For"
COL num_rows         FORMAT 999,999,999 HEADING "Row Count"
COL blocks           FORMAT 999,999 HEADING "# of|Blocks"
COL avg_row_len      FORMAT 9999 HEADING "Avg|Row|Len"
TTITLE "Results of Table Loading|(from DBA_TABLES)"
SELECT
     table_name
    ,tablespace_name
    ,compression
    ,compress_for
    ,num_rows
    ,blocks
    ,avg_row_len
  FROM dba_tables
 WHERE owner = 'AP'
   AND table_name LIKE '%PARTED%'
 ORDER BY 1
;
TTITLE OFF

COL table_name       FORMAT A20 HEADING "Table"
COL partition_name   FORMAT A20 HEADING "Partition"
COL compression      FORMAT A12 HEADING "Compression|Level"
COL compress_for     FORMAT A40 HEADING "Compress|For"
COL num_rows         FORMAT 999,999,999 HEADING "Row Count"
COL blocks           FORMAT 999,999 HEADING "# of|Blocks"
COL avg_row_len      FORMAT 9999 HEADTNG "Avg|Row|Len"
TTITLE "Results of Partitioned Table Loading|(from DBA_TAB_PARTITIONS)"
SELECT
     table_name
    ,partition_name
    ,compression
    ,compress_for
    ,num_rows
    ,blocks
    ,avg_row_len
  FROM dba_tab_partitions
```

```
WHERE table_owner = 'AP'
  AND table_name LIKE '%PARTED%'
ORDER BY 1,2
;
TTITLE OFF
```

SQL@CDB1> @Monitor_ADO_Objects.sql

```
Results of Table Loading (from DBA_TABLES)

Avg
                            Compression Compress                        # of  Row
Table            Tablespace Level       For             Row Count    Blocks  Len
---------------- ---------- ----------- --------------- ------------ ------- ----
RANDOMIZED_PARTED                                          1,000,000   8,056   33

Results of Partitioned Table Loading
(from DBA_TAB_PARTITIONS)

                                                                        Avg
                           Compression Compress                   # of  Row
Table             Partition Level      For          Row Count   Blocks  Len
---------------- ---------- ----------- ----------- ----------- ------- ----
RANDOMIZED_PARTED P1_HOT    DISABLED                     7,988    1,006   33
RANDOMIZED_PARTED P2_WARM   DISABLED                   192,617    2,014   33
RANDOMIZED_PARTED P3_COOL   DISABLED                   300,428    2,014   33
RANDOMIZED_PARTED P4_COLD   DISABLED                   498,967    3,022   33
```

Now activate Heat Mapping for the **PROD_AP** PDB and add new ILM ADO policies just for the **AP.RANDOMIZED_PARTED** table, as shown in **Create_ADO_Policies.sql**.

```
/*
|| Script:  Create_ADO_Policies.sql
|| Purpose: Builds ILM ADO policies for selected objects and partitions
*/


-----
-- Partition:        P1_HOT
-- ILM Policy Level: ROW
-- Compression:      ADVANCED (OLTP)
-- Timeframe:        180 days
-- Basis:            No DML changes
-----
ALTER TABLE ap.randomized_parted
    MODIFY PARTITION p1_hot
    ILM ADD POLICY
        COMPRESS FOR OLTP
        SEGMENT
        AFTER 180 DAYS OF NO MODIFICATION;


-----
-- Partition:        P2_WARM
-- ILM Policy Level: ROW
-- Compression:      ADVANCED (OLTP)
-- Timeframe:        300 days
-- Basis:            Table Scans ONLY
-----
ALTER TABLE ap.randomized_parted
    MODIFY PARTITION p2_warm
    ILM ADD POLICY
        COMPRESS
        SEGMENT
        AFTER 300 DAYS OF NO ACCESS;


-----
-- Partition:        P3_COOL
-- ILM Policy Level: SEGMENT
-- Compression:      STANDARD
-- Timeframe:        600 days
-- Basis:            NO Access
-----
```

```
ALTER TABLE ap.randomized_parted
    MODIFY PARTITION p3_cool
        ILM ADD POLICY
        COMPRESS
        SEGMENT
        AFTER 600 DAYS OF NO ACCESS;

-----
-- Partition:        P4_COLD
-- ILM Policy Level: SEGMENT
-- Compression:      STANDARD
-- Timeframe:        900 days
-- Basis:            NO Access
-----
ALTER TABLE ap.randomized_parted
    MODIFY PARTITION p4_cold
    ILM ADD POLICY
        COMPRESS
        SEGMENT
        AFTER 900 DAYS OF NO ACCESS;
```

```
SQL@CDB1> ALTER SYSTEM SET heat_map = ON;
System altered.

SQL@CDB1> @Create_ADO_Policies.sql
Table altered.
Table altered.
Table altered.
Table altered.
```

We can review the current ADO policies in force by running the queries in script
`Monitor_ADO_Policies.sql`.

```
/*
|| Script:  Monitor_ADO_Policies.sql
|| Purpose: Provides queries against key ILM and Heat Map data dictionary views
||          for reviewing and managing Oracle 12c Automatic Data Optimization
||          (ADO) policies and results of those policies when demonstrating
*/

SET PAGESIZE 2000

/*
|| Viewing ILM Policy Details
*/

SET LINESIZE 80
COL partition_name FORMAT A10 HEADING "Partition|Name"
COL compression FORMAT A12 HEADING "Compression|Level"
COL compress_for FORMAT A10 HEADING "Compress|For"
COL num_rows FORMAT 999,999,999 HEADING "Row Count"
COL blocks    FORMAT 999,999 HEADING "# of|Blocks"
COL avg_row_len FORMAT 9999 HEADING "Avg|Row|Len"
TTITLE "Results of Partitioned Table Loading|(from DBA_TAB_PARTITIONS)"
SELECT
      partition_name
    ,compression
    ,compress_for
    ,num_rows
    ,blocks
    ,avg_row_len
  FROM dba_tab_partitions
 WHERE table_owner = 'AP'
   AND table_name LIKE '%PARTED%'
 ORDER BY 1
```

```
;
TTITLE OFF

-----
-- View ILM Data Movement policies and ILM Policy "inheritance":
-- 1.) Tables inherit tablespace-level policies unless overridden at
table level
-- 2.) Partitions inherit table-level policies unless overridden at
partition level
-- 3.) Different table and partition policies are +additive+
-----

SET LINESIZE 130
COL policy_name FORMAT A06 HEADING "ILM Policy"
COL object_type FORMAT A15 HEADING "Object Type"
COL subobject_name FORMAT A20 HEADING "Subobject|Name"
COL inherited_from FORMAT A20 HEADING "Inheritance"
COL action_type FORMAT A11 HEADING "Action|Type"
COL scope FORMAT A12 HEADING "Scope"
COL compression_level FORMAT A12 HEADING "Compress|Level"
COL tier_tablespace FORMAT A15 HEADING "Tiering|Tablespace"
COL condition_type FORMAT A25 HEADING "Condition Type"
COL condition_days FORMAT 99999 HEADING "Cndtn|Days"
COL custom_function FORMAT A40 HEADING "Custom Function" WRAP
TTITLE "ILM Data Movement Policies|(from DBA_ILMOBJECTS and
DBA_ILMDATAMOVEMENTPOLICIES)"
SELECT
    IO.policy_name
    ,IO.subobject_name
    ,IO.object_type
--  ,IO.inherited_from
    ,IP.action_type
    ,IP.scope
    ,IP.compression_level
    ,IP.tier_tablespace
    ,IP.condition_type
    ,IP.condition_days
--  ,IP.custom_function
  FROM
    dba_ilmobjects IO
    ,dba_ilmdatamovementpolicies IP
  WHERE IO.policy_name = IP.policy_name
  ORDER BY IO.policy_name, IO.subobject_name, IO.object_type
;
TTITLE OFF

/*
|| Viewing ILM Tracking Statistics
*/


-----
-- View statistics for segment-level ILM tracking
-----
COL owner FORMAT A08 HEADING "Table|Owner"
COL table_name FORMAT A20 HEADING "Table Name"
COL activity_tracking FORMAT A20 HEADING "Activity|Tracking"
COL last_dml_dtm FORMAT A20 HEADING "Last DML|Timestamp"
TTITLE "ILM Activity Tracking|(from DBA_TABLES)"
SELECT
    owner
    ,table_name
    ,activity_tracking
    ,TO_CHAR(dml_timestamp, 'yyyy-mm-dd hh24:mi:ss') last_dml_dtm
  FROM dba_tables
  WHERE owner = 'AP'
    AND table_name LIKE '%PARTED%'
;
```

```
TTITLE OFF

/*
|| Viewing ILM Execution Statistics
*/


-----
-- What ILM scheduled tasks exist?
-----
COL task_id FORMAT 999999 HEADING "TaskID"
COL task_owner FORMAT A12 HEADING "Task|Owner"
COL state FORMAT A10 HEADING "Task|State"
COL creation_dtm FORMAT A19 HEADING "Created On"
COL start_dtm FORMAT A19 HEADING "Started At"
COL finish_dtm FORMAT A19 HEADING "Ended At"
TTITLE "ILM Scheduled Tasks In Last 24 Hours|(from DBA_ILMTASKS)"
SELECT
      task_id
    ,task_owner
    ,state
    ,TO_CHAR(creation_time, 'yyyy-mm-dd hh24:mi:ss') creation_dtm
    ,TO_CHAR(start_time, 'yyyy-mm-dd hh24:mi:ss') start_dtm
    ,TO_CHAR(completion_time, 'yyyy-mm-dd hh24:mi:ss') finish_dtm
  FROM dba_ilmtasks
  WHERE creation_time >= (SYSDATE - 1)
 ORDER BY start_time DESC
;
TTITLE OFF


-----
-- What's the status of ILM scheduled task executions?
-----
COL task_id FORMAT 999999 HEADING "Task|ID"
COL job_name FORMAT A10 HEADING "Job|Name"
COL job_state FORMAT A24 HEADING "Job|State"
COL task_owner FORMAT A12 HEADING "Task|Owner"
COL start_dtm FORMAT A19 HEADING "Started At"
COL finish_dtm FORMAT A19 HEADING "Ended At"
TTITLE "ILM Scheduled Tasks Execution Status|(from DBA_ILMRESULTS)"
SELECT
      task_id
    ,job_name
    ,job_state
    ,TO_CHAR(start_time, 'yyyy-mm-dd hh24:mi:ss') start_dtm
    ,TO_CHAR(completion_time, 'yyyy-mm-dd hh24:mi:ss') finish_dtm
--    ,comments
--    ,statistics
  FROM dba_ilmresults
  WHERE start_time >= (SYSDATE - 1)
 ORDER BY task_id DESC
;
TTITLE OFF


-----
-- Which ILM evaluation tasks have occurred?
-----
COL task_id FORMAT 9999 HEADING "Task|ID"
COL policy_name FORMAT A06 HEADING "ILM|Policy"
COL object_owner FORMAT A06 HEADING "Object|Owner"
COL object_name FORMAT A20 HEADING "Object Name"
COL subobject_name FORMAT A20 HEADING "Subobject|Name"
COL object_type FORMAT A15 HEADING "Object Type"
COL picked FORMAT A30 HEADING "Reason Chosen"
COL job_name FORMAT A10 HEADING "Job Name"
TTITLE "ILM Objects Most Recently Evaluated|(from
DBA_ILMEVALUATIONDETAILS)"
SELECT
```

```
         task_id
        ,policy_name
        ,object_owner
        ,object_name
        ,subobject_name
        ,object_type
        ,selected_for_execution picked
        ,job_name
--      ,comments
  FROM dba_ilmevaluationdetails
 WHERE object_owner = 'AP'
   AND object_name like '%PARTED%'
 ORDER BY task_id DESC
;
TTITLE OFF

SET LINESIZE 40
COL tablespace_name FORMAT A15 HEADING "Tablespace|Name"
COL used_mb FORMAT 999999 HEADING "Free|Space|(MB)"
TTITLE "Tablespace Size|(from DBA_FREE_SPACE)"
SELECT
       tablespace_name
      ,ROUND((SUM(bytes) / (1024*1024)),2) used_mb
  FROM dba_free_space
 WHERE tablespace_name LIKE 'ADO%DATA%'
 GROUP BY tablespace_name
 ORDER BY tablespace_name
;
TTITLE OFF
```

Note that even though ILM ADO policies have been created, as of yet they have not been evaluated for any required action.

```
SQL@CDB1> @Monitor_ADO_Policies.sql
```

```
ILM Data Movement Policies
(from DBA_ILMOBJECTS and DBA_ILMDATAMOVEMENTPOLICIES)
```

ILM Po	Subobject Name	Object Type	Action Type	Scope	Compress Level	Condition Type	Cndtn Days
P1	P1_HOT	TABLE PARTITION	COMPRESSION	ROW	ADVANCED	LAST MODIFICATION TIME	180
P21	P2_WARM	TABLE PARTITION	COMPRESSION	SEGMENT		LAST ACCESS TIME	300
P22	P3_COOL	TABLE PARTITION	COMPRESSION	SEGMENT		LAST ACCESS TIME	600
P23	P4_COLD	TABLE PARTITION	COMPRESSION	SEGMENT		LAST ACCESS TIME	900

To demonstrate how heat mapping actually works, we'll connect to the PROD_AP database as the AP user account, execute some DML, and perform queries against several of the partitions of AP.RANDOMIZED_PARTED, as the code in Modify_ADO_Data.sql shows.

```
/*
|| Script:  Modify_ADO_Data.sql
|| Purpose: Accesses ADO objects prior to ILM ADO policy evaluation
*/

SET SERVEROUTPUT ON
DECLARE
    cur_max NUMBER := 0;
    new_max NUMBER := 0;
    ctr NUMBER := 0;
BEGIN
    SELECT MAX(key_id)
      INTO cur_max
      FROM ap.randomized_parted;
    cur_max := cur_max + 1;
    new_max := cur_max + 50000;
    FOR ctr IN cur_max..new_max
```

```
          LOOP
              INSERT INTO ap.randomized_parted
              VALUES(ctr
                  ,(TO_DATE('12/31/2016','mm/dd/yyyy')
                    + DBMS_RANDOM.VALUE(1,90))
                  ,'NEWHOTROW'
                  ,20
              );
              IF MOD(ctr, 5000) = 0 THEN
                  COMMIT;
              END IF;
          END LOOP;
          COMMIT;
EXCEPTION
     WHEN OTHERS THEN
        DBMS_OUTPUT.PUT_LINE('Fatal Error: ' || SQLERRM);
END;
/

UPDATE ap.randomized_parted
   SET key_desc = 'Modified *** MODIFIED!!!'
 WHERE key_desc <> 'Modified *** MODIFIED!!!'
   AND key_date BETWEEN TO_DATE('2016-12-01','YYYY-MM-DD')
                    AND TO_DATE('2016-12-31','YYYY-MM-DD')
   AND ROWNUM < 50001;

COMMIT;

SELECT MAX(LENGTH(key_desc)), COUNT(key_sts)
   FROM ap.randomized_parted
 WHERE key_date BETWEEN TO_DATE('2015-03-15','YYYY-MM-DD')
                    AND TO_DATE('2016-11-30','YYYY-MM-DD')
   AND ROWNUM < 10001;

SELECT MAX(LENGTH(key_desc)), COUNT(key_sts)
   FROM ap.randomized_parted
 WHERE key_date BETWEEN TO_DATE('2014-03-15','YYYY-MM-DD')
                    AND TO_DATE('2014-04-14','YYYY-MM-DD')
   AND ROWNUM < 10001;

SELECT MAX(LENGTH(key_desc)), COUNT(key_sts)
   FROM ap.randomized_parted
 WHERE key_date BETWEEN TO_DATE('2009-07-15','YYYY-MM-DD')
                    AND TO_DATE('2013-06-30','YYYY-MM-DD')
   AND ROWNUM < 10001;

SQL@CDB1> CONNECT ap/ap@prod_ap
Connected.

SQL@CDB1> @Modify_ADO_Data.sql
50000 rows inserted.
Commit complete.

7988 rows updated.
Commit completed.

MAX(LENGTH(KEY_DESC)) COUNT(KEY_STS)
-------------------- --------------
                  31          10000
. . .
```

We can see the impact of executing these statements by querying several views that contain Heat Map data, using `Monitor_HeatMaps.sql` to show this information.

```
/*
|| Script:  Monitor_HeatMaps.sql
|| Purpose: Shows current state of Heat Maps
*/

SET LINESIZE 130
SET PAGESIZE 2000


-----
-- Which ILM-managed segments have been "touched" since the last
instance restart?
-----
SET LINESIZE 130
COL object_name FORMAT A30 HEADING "Object Name"
COL subobject_name FORMAT A30 HEADING "Subobject Name"
COL track_dtm FORMAT A30 HEADING "Last|Time|Tracked"
COL segment_write FORMAT A06 HEADING "Sgmt|Wrtn"
COL segment_read FORMAT A06 HEADING "Sgmt|Read"
COL full_scan FORMAT A06 HEADING "Full|Scan"
COL lookup_scan FORMAT A06 HEADING "Sgmt|Lookup"
TTITLE "Recently-Touched Segments|(from V$HEAT_MAP_SEGMENT)"
SELECT
      object_name
     ,subobject_name
     ,TO_CHAR(track_time, 'yyyy-mm-dd hh24:mi:ss') track_dtm
     ,segment_write
     ,segment_read
     ,full_scan
     ,lookup_scan
  FROM v$heat_map_segment
 WHERE object_name like '%PARTED%'
 ORDER BY object_name, subobject_name
;
TTITLE OFF


-----
-- Which ILM-managed segments have been "touched" and how have they
been touched?
-----
SET LINESIZE 130
COL owner FORMAT A06 HEADING "Object|Owner"
COL object_name FORMAT A25 HEADING "Object Name"
COL subobject_name FORMAT A25 HEADING "Subobject Name"
COL last_touch_dtm FORMAT A19 HEADING "Last Touched"
COL seg_wts FORMAT A08 HEADING "Segment|Wrtn To?"
COL seg_fts FORMAT A08 HEADING "Segment|FTS?"
COL seg_lkp FORMAT A08 HEADING "Segment|LKP?"
TTITLE "Recently-Touched Segments(from DBA_HEAT_MAP_SEG_HISTOGRAM)"
SELECT
      owner
     ,object_name
     ,subobject_name
     ,TO_CHAR(track_time, 'yyyy-mm-dd hh24:mi:ss') last_touch_dtm
     ,segment_write seg_wts
     ,full_scan seg_fts
     ,lookup_scan seg_lkp
  FROM dba_heat_map_seg_histogram
 WHERE owner IN ('AP', 'OE')
   AND object_name like '%PARTED%'
 ORDER BY TO_CHAR(track_time, 'yyyy-mm-dd hh24:mi:ss') DESC, owner,
object_name, subobject_name
;
TTITLE OFF


-----
```

```
-- Which ILM-managed segments have been "touched" most recently, and
when?
-----
SET LINESIZE 150
COL owner FORMAT A06 HEADING "Object|Owner"
COL object_name FORMAT A25 HEADING "Object Name"
COL subobject_name FORMAT A25 HEADING "Subobject Name"
COL seg_wrt_dtm FORMAT A19 HEADING "Segment|Last Written"
COL seg_rd_dtm FORMAT A19 HEADING "Segment|Last Read"
COL seg_fts_dtm FORMAT A19 HEADING "Segment|Last FTS"
COL seg_lkp_dtm FORMAT A19 HEADING "Segment|Last Accessed"
TTITLE "Recently-Touched Segments(from DBA_HEAT_MAP_SEGMENT)"
SELECT
     owner
    ,object_name
    ,subobject_name
    ,TO_CHAR(segment_write_time, 'yyyy-mm-dd hh24:mi:ss') seg_wrt_dtm
    ,TO_CHAR(segment_read_time, 'yyyy-mm-dd hh24:mi:ss') seg_rd_dtm
    ,TO_CHAR(full_scan, 'yyyy-mm-dd hh24:mi:ss') seg_fts_dtm
    ,TO_CHAR(lookup_scan, 'yyyy-mm-dd hh24:mi:ss') seg_lkp_dtm
  FROM dba_heat_map_segment
 WHERE owner IN ('AP','OE')
   AND object_name like '%PARTED%'
 ORDER BY owner, object_name, subobject_name
;
TTITLE OFF

/*
-----
-- What are the hottest segments?
-----
SET LINESIZE 130
COL owner FORMAT A12 HEADING "Object|Owner"
COL object_name FORMAT A30 HEADING "Object Name"
COL tablespace_name FORMAT A30 HEADING "Tablespace"
COL segment_count FORMAT 999999 HEADING "Segment|Count"
COL object_size FORMAT 999999 HEADING "Object|Size"
COL min_wrtn_dtm FORMAT A19 HEADING "Earliest|Write Time"
COL min_read_dtm FORMAT A19 HEADING "Earliest|Read Time"
COL min_fts_dtm FORMAT A19 HEADING "Earliest|FTS Time"
COL min_lkp_dtm FORMAT A19 HEADING "Earliest|Lookup Time"
COL avg_wrtn_dtm FORMAT A19 HEADING "Average|Write Time"
COL avg_read_dtm FORMAT A19 HEADING "Average|Read Time"
COL avg_fts_dtm FORMAT A19 HEADING "Average|FTS Time"
COL avg_lkp_dtm FORMAT A19 HEADING "Average|Lookup Time"
COL max_wrtn_dtm FORMAT A19 HEADING "Latest|Write Time"
COL max_read_dtm FORMAT A19 HEADING "Latest|Read Time"
COL max_fts_dtm FORMAT A19 HEADING "Latest|FTS Time"
COL max_lkp_dtm FORMAT A19 HEADING "Latest|Lookup Time"
TTITLE "Hottest Segments|(from DBA_HEATMAP_TOP_OBJECTS)"
SELECT
     owner
    ,object_name
    ,object_type
    ,tablespace_name
    ,segment_count
    ,object_size
    ,TO_CHAR(min_writetime, 'yyyy-mm-dd.hh24:mi:ss') min_wrtn_dtm
    ,TO_CHAR(min_readtime, 'yyyy-mm-dd.hh24:mi:ss') min_read_dtm
    ,TO_CHAR(min_ftstime, 'yyyy-mm-dd.hh24:mi:ss') min_fts_dtm
    ,TO_CHAR(min_lookuptime, 'yyyy-mm-dd.hh24:mi:ss') min_lkp_dtm
    ,TO_CHAR(avg_writetime, 'yyyy-mm-dd.hh24:mi:ss') avg_wrtn_dtm
    ,TO_CHAR(avg_readtime, 'yyyy-mm-dd.hh24:mi:ss') avg_read_dtm
    ,TO_CHAR(avg_ftstime, 'yyyy-mm-dd.hh24:mi:ss') avg_fts_dtm
    ,TO_CHAR(avg_lookuptime, 'yyyy-mm-dd.hh24:mi:ss') avg_lkp_dtm
    ,TO_CHAR(max_writetime, 'yyyy-mm-dd.hh24:mi:ss') max_wrtn_dtm
    ,TO_CHAR(max_readtime, 'yyyy-mm-dd.hh24:mi:ss') max_read_dtm
```

```
       ,TO_CHAR(max_ftstime, 'yyyy-mm-dd.hh24:mi:ss') max_fts_dtm
       ,TO_CHAR(max_lookuptime, 'yyyy-mm-dd.hh24:mi:ss') max_lkp_dtm
  FROM dba_heatmap_top_objects
WHERE owner IN ('AP','OE')
  AND object_name like '%PARTED%'
 ORDER BY owner, object_name
;
TTITLE OFF
*/


-----
-- What are the hottest tablespaces?
-----
SET LINESIZE 120
COL tablespace_name FORMAT A15 HEADING "Tablespace|Name"
COL alloc_mb FORMAT 999999 HEADING "Alloc|Space|(MB)"
COL segment_count FORMAT 999999 HEADING "Segment|Count"
COL max_wrtn_dtm FORMAT A19 HEADING "Latest|Write Time"
COL max_read_dtm FORMAT A19 HEADING "Latest|Read Time"
COL max_fts_dtm FORMAT A19 HEADING "Latest|FTS Time"
COL max_lkp_dtm FORMAT A19 HEADING "Latest|Lookup Time"
TTITLE "Hottest Tablespaces|(from DBA_HEATMAP_TOP_TABLESPACES)"
SELECT
      tablespace_name
     ,segment_count
     ,(allocated_bytes / (1024*1024)) alloc_mb
     ,TO_CHAR(max_writetime, 'yyyy-mm-dd.hh24:mi:ss') max_wrtn_dtm
     ,TO_CHAR(max_readtime, 'yyyy-mm-dd.hh24:mi:ss') max_read_dtm
     ,TO_CHAR(max_ftstime, 'yyyy-mm-dd.hh24:mi:ss') max_fts_dtm
     ,TO_CHAR(max_lookuptime, 'yyyy-mm-dd.hh24:mi:ss') max_lkp_dtm
  FROM dba_heatmap_top_tablespaces
 ORDER BY tablespace_name
;
TTITLE OFF
```

```
SQL@CDB1> @Monitor_HeatMaps.sql

Recently-Touched Segments
(from V$HEAT_MAP_SEGMENT)
                                           Last
                                           Time              Sgmt  Sgmt  Full  Sgmt
Object Name           Subobject Name Tracked               Wrtn  Read  Scan  Lookup
-------------------   -------------- -------------------   ----- ----- ----- ------
RANDOMIZED_PARTED     P1_HOT         2017-06-24 14:13:53   YES   NO    YES   NO
RANDOMIZED_PARTED     P2_WARM        2017-06-24 14:13:53   NO    NO    YES   NO
RANDOMIZED_PARTED     P3_COOL        2017-06-24 14:13:53   NO    NO    YES   NO
RANDOMIZED_PARTED     P4_COLD        2017-06-24 14:13:53   NO    NO    YES   NO

Recently-Touched Segments(from DBA_HEAT_MAP_SEG_HISTOGRAM)

Object                                                     Segment  Segment  Segment
Owner  Object Name    Subobject Name Last Touched          Wrtn To? FTS?     LKP?
------ -------------- -------------- -------------------   -------- -------- -------
AP     RANDOMIZED_PARTED  P1_HOT     2017-06-24 14:13:53 YES   YES      NO
AP     RANDOMIZED_PARTED  P2_WARM    2017-06-24 14:13:53 NO    YES      NO
AP     RANDOMIZED_PARTED  P3_COOL    2017-06-24 14:13:53 NO    YES      NO
AP     RANDOMIZED_PARTED  P4_COLD    2017-06-24 14:13:53 NO    YES      NO

Recently-Touched Segments(from DBA_HEAT_MAP_SEGMENT)

Object                                Segment              Segment              Segment              Segment
Owner  Object Name    Subobject Name Last Written          Last Read            Last FTS             Last
Accessed
------ -------------- -------------- -------------------  -------------------  -------------------  ---------
AP     RANDOMIZED_PARTED  P1_HOT     2017-06-24 14:13:53                        2017-06-24 14:13:53
AP     RANDOMIZED_PARTED  P2_WARM                                               2017-06-24 14:13:53
AP     RANDOMIZED_PARTED  P3_COOL                                               2017-06-24 14:13:53
AP     RANDOMIZED_PARTED  P4_COLD                                               2017-06-24 14:13:53
```

Before we request ILM to evaluate these policies, let's temporarily switch the ILM evaluation mode to treat any ILM ADO policy that would normally wait for a number of days to elapse before implementing the policy, to instead wait for the same number of seconds.

```
/*
|| Script:  Modify_ILM_Policy_Time.sql
|| Purpose: Switches ILM policy evaluation timeframe thresholds so that
policy
||          days are treated as seconds instead.
*/
BEGIN
    DBMS_ILM_ADMIN.CUSTOMIZE_ILM(
        parameter => DBMS_ILM_ADMIN.POLICY_TIME
        ,value => DBMS_ILM_ADMIN.ILM_POLICY_IN_SECONDS);
    DBMS_ILM_ADMIN.CUSTOMIZE_ILM(
        parameter => DBMS_ILM_ADMIN.EXECUTION_INTERVAL
        ,value => 3);
END;
/
```

```
SQL@CDB1> @Modify_ILM_Policy_Time.sql
PL/SQL procedure complete.
```

Now, let's request ILM to evaluate the ADO policies. We'll leverage the code in `Execute_ILM_Tasks.sql` to do that.

```
/*
|| Script:  Execute_ILM_Tasks.sql
|| Purpose: Invokes tasks to evaluate ILM ADO policies
*/
DECLARE
    tid NUMBER;
BEGIN
    DBMS_ILM.EXECUTE_ILM(owner => 'AP', object_name =>
'RANDOMIZED_PARTED', task_id => tid);
END;
/
```

```
SQL@CDB1> @Execute_ILM_Tasks.sql
PL/SQL procedure complete.
```

To see what ILM ADO policies have been triggered by the evaluation request, let's run the queries in `Monitor_ADO_Policies.sql` once again.

```
SQL@CDB1> @Monitor_ADO_Policies.sql
```

```
ILM Data Movement Policies
(from DBA_ILMOBJECTS and DBA_ILMDATAMOVEMENTPOLICIES)
         Subobject                         Action              Compress                              Cndtn
ILM Po  Name            Object Type        Type     Scope      Level     Condition Type              Days
------  ------------    ---------------    -------  ---------  --------  -----------------------     -----
P1      P1_HOT          TABLE PARTITION    COMPRESSION ROW                ADVANCED  LAST MODIFICATION TIME   180
P21     P2_WARM         TABLE PARTITION    COMPRESSION SEGMENT                      LAST ACCESS TIME         300
P22     P3_COOL         TABLE PARTITION    COMPRESSION SEGMENT                      LAST ACCESS TIME         600
P23     P4_COLD         TABLE PARTITION    COMPRESSION SEGMENT                      LAST ACCESS TIME         900

ILM Scheduled Tasks In Last 24 Hours
(from DBA_ILMTASKS)
          Task          Task
TaskID   Owner         State      Created On            Started At            Ended At
------   -----         ---------  -------------------   -------------------   -------------------
    9    SYS           COMPLETED  2017-06-23 18:23:14   2017-06-23 18:23:14   2017-06-23 18:23:25
    8    SYS           COMPLETED  2017-06-23 18:20:31   2017-06-23 18:20:31   2017-06-23 18:20:31
    . . .
```

```
ILM Scheduled Tasks Execution Status
(from DBA_ILMRESULTS)

 Task Job           Job
   ID Name          State                     Started At            Ended At
----- ----------    ----------------------    --------------------  --------------------
    9 ILMJOB5126    COMPLETED SUCCESSFULLY    2017-06-23 18:23:20   2017-06-23 18:23:25

ILM Objects Most Recently Evaluated
(from DBA_ILMEVALUATIONDETAILS)

 Task ILM   Object                            Subobject
   ID Policy Owner  Object Name                Name      Object Type      Reason Chosen                 Job Name
----- ------ -----  -----------------------    --------  ---------------  --------------------------    ----------
    9 P21    AP     RANDOMIZED_PARTED          P2_WARM   TABLE PARTITION  STATISTICS NOT AVAILABLE
    9 P22    AP     RANDOMIZED_PARTED          P3_COOL   TABLE PARTITION  STATISTICS NOT AVAILABLE
    9 P23    AP     RANDOMIZED_PARTED          P4_COLD   TABLE PARTITION  STATISTICS NOT AVAILABLE
    9 P1     AP     RANDOMIZED_PARTED          P1_HOT    TABLE PARTITION  SELECTED FOR EXECUTION        ILMJOB5126
```

Finally, let's run the queries in `Monitor_ADO_Objects.sql` to see what happened to the "coldest" segments of `AP.RANDOMIZED_PARTED`.

`SQL@CDB1> @Monitor_ADO_Policies.sql`

```
Results of Partitioned Table Loading
(from DBA_TAB_PARTITIONS)
                                                                                   Avg
                                          Compression Compress                # of Row
Table                    Partition        Level       For          Row Count  Blocks Len
-----------------------  ---------------  ----------- ---------    ---------  ------ ---
RANDOMIZED_PARTED        P1_HOT           ENABLED     ADVANCED        57,989   1,006  29
RANDOMIZED_PARTED        P2_WARM          ENABLED     BASIC          192,617   2,014  33
RANDOMIZED_PARTED        P3_COOL          ENABLED     BASIC          300,428   2,014  33
RANDOMIZED_PARTED        P4_COLD          ENABLED     BASIC          498,967   3,022  33
```

We should see that at least one ILM policy has been triggered – most likely, against the `P1_HOT` partition of `AP.RANDOMIZED_PARTED` – but if not, simply wait a few more minutes and then repeat again. Remember that since we've requested ILM to treat a day as if it's really just a second, it may take as long as 15 minutes (i.e. **900** seconds) to see an impact on the "coldest" partition (`P4_COLD`).

BONUS: If you regather statistics on the `AP.RANDOMIZED_PARTED` table after all ILM ADO evaluations have occurred, you will see the true benefit of these policies. - A significant reduction in the number of blocks (and therefore the *size*) of the four partitions, as the results from the same query show here.

```
Results of Partitioned Table Loading
(from DBA_TAB_PARTITIONS)
Avg
                                          Compression Compress                # of Row
Table                    Partition        Level       For          Row Count  Blocks Len
-----------------------  ---------------  ----------- ---------    ---------  ------ ---
RANDOMIZED_PARTED        P1_HOT           ENABLED     ADVANCED        57,831     178  29
RANDOMIZED_PARTED        P2_WARM          ENABLED     BASIC          191,342     847  33
RANDOMIZED_PARTED        P3_COOL          ENABLED     BASIC          301,452   1,340  33
RANDOMIZED_PARTED        P4_COLD          ENABLED     BASIC          499,376   2,212  33
```

10.   Appendices

Fundamentals of PDBs That Every DBA Needs to Know

Connecting to a CDB or root container (CDB$ROOT)

Every DBA new to the PDB world seem to struggle for the first week of their journey establishing connectivity to PDBs. In this section, we will address the common methods of connection to CDB/PDB. Understanding how to connect to the CDB/PDB will significantly reduce your initial pain points with working with PDBs.

Let's start with connecting to the CDB/root container using OS authentication.

```
$> echo $ORACLE_SID
vnadbnw

$> sqlplus / as sysdba
SQL*Plus: Release 12.2.0.1.0 Production on Sat Aug 12 15:41:26 2017
Copyright (c) 1982, 2016, Oracle.  All rights reserved.
Connected to:
Oracle Database 12c Enterprise Edition Release 12.2.0.1.0 - 64bit
Production

SQL> show con_name
CON_NAME
------------------------------
CDB$ROOT

SQL> show con_id
CON_ID
------------------------------
1
```

As you connect to the database using the SYSDBA role, you are connecting to the root container which happens to have the container ID of 1.

Connect to the PDB Using Easy Connect Method

Connecting to the PDB leveraging the Easy Connect Method will be one of the easiest way to connect to a PDB. You do not have to make any tnsnames.ora entries. You will simply leverage the hostname, port, and the service name associated with the PDB.

```
$> sqlplus sys/oracle123@localhost:1521/vnadb1pdb1 as sysdba
SQL*Plus: Release 12.2.0.1.0 Production on Sat Aug 12 15:57:00 2017
Copyright (c) 1982, 2016, Oracle.  All rights reserved.
Connected to:
Oracle Database 12c Enterprise Edition Release 12.2.0.1.0 - 64bit
Production

SQL> show con_id
CON_ID
------------------------------
3
```

```
SQL> show con_name
CON_NAME
-------------------------------
VNADB1PDB1

SQL> show pdbs
    CON_ID CON_NAME                       OPEN MODE  RESTRICTED
---------- ------------------------------ ---------- ----------
         3 VNADB1PDB1                      READ WRITE NO

SQL> alter session set container=CDB$ROOT;
Session altered.
```

This example leverages the localhost as the hostname. Simply substitute the localhost with the hostname or IP that houses the container database. You will need to know the services name that is associated with the PDB.

Connecting to a PDB Using TNS

We need to create an entry in the tnsnames.ora file to connect leveraging the TNS entry. In our example, we will leverage the vnadb1pdb1 TNS entry.

```
VNADB1PDB1 =
  (DESCRIPTION =
    (ADDRESS = (PROTOCOL = TCP)(HOST = vna01)(PORT = 1521))
    (ADDRESS = (PROTOCOL = TCP)(HOST = vna01)(PORT = 1522))
    (CONNECT_DATA =
      (SERVER = DEDICATED)
      (SERVICE_NAME = vnadb1pdb1)
    )
  )
```

After we create or modify the **tnsnames.ora** entry, we can leverage the TNS alias to connect to the PDB with SQL*Plus.

```
$> sqlplus sys/oracle123@vnadb1pdb1 as sysdba
SQL*Plus: Release 12.2.0.1.0 Production on Sat Aug 12 16:08:04 2017
Copyright (c) 1982, 2016, Oracle.  All rights reserved.
Connected to:
Oracle Database 12c Enterprise Edition Release 12.2.0.1.0 - 64bit
Production

SQL> show con_name

CON_NAME
-------------------------------
VNADB1PDB1

SQL> show con_id

CON_ID
-------------------------------
3
```

Connecting Directly to PBD Using TWO_TASK

Setting TWO_TASK is not the preferred method to connect to the database, but simplifies connectivity. By setting the TWO_TASK environment variable, we can directly connect to the PDB. Just remember to unset the TWO_TASK environment variable for the next environment.

```
$> export TWO_TASK=VNADB1PDB2;

$> sqlplus system

SQL*Plus: Release 12.2.0.1.0 Production on Tue Aug 22 00:24:28 2017

Copyright (c) 1982, 2016, Oracle.  All rights reserved.

Enter password:
Last Successful login time: Tue Aug 22 2017 00:23:47 +01:00

Connected to:
Oracle Database 12c Enterprise Edition Release 12.2.0.1.0 - 64bit
Production

SQL> show con_name

CON_NAME
------------------------------
VNADB1PDB2
```

Starting and Shutting Down CDBs and PDBs

The **STARTUP** and **SHUTDOWN** commands for a CDB are the same as the traditional non-CDB database.

Startup of PDBs can be executed at the container level (**CDB$ROOT**) or they can be done when connected at OS level with the **SYSDBA** role.

```
SQL> alter pluggable database VNADB1PDB2,VNADB1PDB3 open read write;
Pluggable database altered.
```

Also, we can start up or shut down multiple PDBs at the same time. The example below shuts down three PDBs at the same time.

```
SQL> alter pluggable database VNADB1PDB2,VNADB1PDB3 close immediate;
Pluggable database altered.
```

```
SQL> alter pluggable database all open;
Pluggable database altered.

SQL> show pdbs
    CON_ID CON_NAME                        OPEN MODE  RESTRICTED
---------- ------------------------------- ---------- ----------
         2 PDB$SEED                        READ ONLY  NO
         3 VNADB1PDB1                      READ WRITE NO
         4 VNADB1PDB2                      READ WRITE NO
         5 VNADB1PDB3                      READ WRITE NO
```

We can also open all the PDBs within a CDB with a single command.

```
SQL> alter pluggable database all except VNADB1PDB2 close immediate;
Pluggable database altered.
```

```
CDB$ROOT@VNADBNW> show pdbs

    CON_ID CON_NAME                        OPEN MODE  RESTRICTED
---------- ------------------------------- ---------- ----------
         2 PDB$SEED                        READ ONLY  NO
         3 VNADB1PDB1                      MOUNTED
         4 VNADB1PDB2                      READ WRITE NO
         5 VNADB1PDB3                      MOUNTED
```

With the EXCEPT clause, we can exclude one or more PDBs from starting up. Here are some additional derivations of the ALTER PLUGGABLE DATABASE commands.

```
ALTER PLUGGABLE DATABASE ALL CLOSE IMMEDIATE;
ALTER PLUGGABLE DATABASE ALL EXCEPT PDB1 OPEN READ WRITE;
ALTER PLUGGABLE DATABASE ALL OPEN READ WRITE;
```

Executing a Script Across Multiple Pluggable Databases

We can execute SQL scripts or SQL statements across all the PDBs with a perl script that Oracle provided with Oracle 12.1.0.2 release. The perl script, $ORACLE_HOME/perl/bin/perl $ORACLE_HOME/rdbms/admin/catcon.pl, provides this capability to execute the same SQL script or statement across multiple PDBs or all PDBs.

In the example below, we want to query for the tablespace_name for PDB JOHNSPDB2. The output file will be written to /tmp directory, and the names of the files will start with undo_check*. Help on the script options are available in the script.

```
$> $ORACLE_HOME/perl/bin/perl $ORACLE_HOME/rdbms/admin/catcon.pl -u
SYSTEM -U SYSTEM -c JOHNSPDB2 -l /tmp -b undo_check -- --x"select
tablespace_name from dba_tablespaces where contents='UNDO'"

catcon: ALL catcon-related output will be written to [/tmp/undo_check_catcon_10172.lst]
catcon: See [/tmp/undo_check*.log] files for output generated by scripts
catcon: See [/tmp/undo_check_*.lst] files for spool files, if any
Enter Password:
Enter Password:
catcon.pl: completed successfully
```

Log files are generated under /tmp/undo_check*.

```
$> ls -l /tmp/undo_check*
-rw-r--r--. 1 oracle oinstall 2109 May 26 09:22 /tmp/undo_check0.log
-rw-r--r--. 1 oracle oinstall  461 May 26 09:22 /tmp/undo_check1.log
-rw-r--r--. 1 oracle oinstall  559 May 26 09:22 /tmp/undo_check_catcon_10061.lst
```

Manipulating the SQL Prompt to Display the Current PDB

The global login script that executes for SQL*Plus resides in the $ORACLE_HOME/sqlplus/admin directory. Below is a sample glogin script to display the SQL prompt for the connected db name in SQL*Plus. Also, you can use the switch_cont.sql script to switch between PDBS or CDBs.

glogin.sql

```
define gname=idle
column global_name new_value gname
set heading off
```

```
set termout off
col global_name noprint
select upper(sys_context ('userenv', 'con_name') || '@' ||
sys_context('userenv', 'db_name')) global_name from dual;
set sqlprompt '&gname> '
set heading on
set termout on
```

Switch_cont.sql ($ORACLE_HOME/sqlplus/admin directory)

This script will re-execute the glogin.sql script from $ORACLE_HOME/sqlplus/admin directory. The ? designates the value for $ORACLE_HOME in SQL*Plus.

```
set termout off
alter session set container=&1;
@?/sqlplus/admin/glogin.sql
set termout on
```

Enforcing a PDB's Saved State

PDBs do not start up by default when you start a CDB. If you want to automate the startup of PDBs, execute the ALTER PLUGGABLE DATABASE command with the SAVE STATE clause. Below is an example that displays that PDBs do not start up by default without setting the saved state. Once we save the state of the pluggable database when they were open, PDBs will continue to open in READ WRITE mode. We can save the state of *each* PDB or save the state for *all* the PDBs in a single command.

```
$> sqlplus / as sysdba

SQL*Plus: Release 12.2.0.1.0 Production on Tue Aug 15 18:26:57 2017

Copyright (c) 1982, 2016, Oracle.  All rights reserved.


Connected to:
Oracle Database 12c Enterprise Edition Release 12.2.0.1.0 - 64bit
Production
SQL> show pdbs

    CON_ID CON_NAME                       OPEN MODE  RESTRICTED
---------- ------------------------------ ---------- ----------
         2 PDB$SEED                       READ ONLY  NO
         3 VNADB1PDB1                     MOUNTED
         4 VNADB1PDB2                     MOUNTED
         5 VNADB1PDB3                     MOUNTED

SQL> @switch_cont VNADB1PDB1

SQL> select username from dba_users;
select username from dba_users
                         *
ERROR at line 1:
ORA-01219: database or pluggable database not open: queries allowed on fixed
tables or views only

SQL> @switch_cont CDB$ROOT
SQL> alter pluggable database all open;
```

```
Pluggable database altered.

SQL> select a.name,b.state from v$pdbs a , dba_pdb_saved_states b where
a.con_id = b.con_id;
no rows selected

SQL> alter pluggable database all save state;
Pluggable database altered.

SQL> select a.name,b.state from v$pdbs a , dba_pdb_saved_states b where
a.con_id = b.con_id;

NAME             STATE
--------------   ------
VNADB1PDB1       OPEN
VNADB1PDB3       OPEN
VNADB1PDB2       OPEN

SQL> shutdown immediate

Database closed.
Database dismounted.
ORACLE instance shut down.

SQL> startup
ORACLE instance started.
Total System Global Area 8.1068E+10 bytes
Fixed Size                 30036880 bytes
Variable Size            1.3153E+10 bytes
Database Buffers         6.7646E+10 bytes
Redo Buffers              238395392 bytes
Database mounted.
Database opened.

SQL> show pdbs

    CON_ID CON_NAME                            OPEN MODE   RESTRICTED
---------- --------------------------------    ----------  ----------
         2 PDB$SEED                            READ ONLY   NO
         3 VNADB1PDB1                          READ WRITE  NO
         4 VNADB1PDB2                          READ WRITE  NO
         5 VNADB1PDB3                          READ WRITE  NO
```

Similarly, we can also wipe out the existing persistency of the PDB. With the ALTER PLUGGABLE DATABASE command, we can issue the DISCARD STATE clause to unset the persistency of the PDB at CDB startup.

```
SQL> alter pluggable database all discard state;

Pluggable database altered.

SQL> shutdown immediate
Database closed.
Database dismounted.
ORACLE instance shut down.

SQL> startup
ORACLE instance started.

Total System Global Area 8.1068E+10 bytes
Fixed Size                 30036880 bytes
Variable Size            1.3153E+10 bytes
Database Buffers         6.7646E+10 bytes
Redo Buffers              238395392 bytes
Database mounted.
Database opened.
```

```
SQL> show pdbs

    CON_ID CON_NAME                                          OPEN MODE   RESTRICTED
---------- ------------------------------------------------  ----------  ----------
         2 PDB$SEED                                          READ ONLY   NO
         3 VNADB1PDB1                                        MOUNTED
         4 VNADB1PDB2                                        MOUNTED
         5 VNADB1PDB3                                        MOUNTED
```

By unsetting the persistency of the PDBs, all the PDBs are in MOUNTED mode at CDB startup.

Finally, even though we can preserve the state of the PDB for future persistence the majority of the time, we will want all the databases to start as part of the CDB startup process. Review the sample code of a database trigger that will start up all the PDBs when the database starts up below.

```
CREATE OR REPLACE TRIGGER AFTER_STARTUP
AFTER STARTUP ON DATABASE
BEGIN
EXECUTE IMMEDIATE 'ALTER PLUGGABLE DATABASE ALL OPEN';
END AFTER_STARTUP;
/
SHOW ERRORS;
```

Additional Helpful PDB Scripts

Feel free to leverage these utility scripts that can help make short work of everyday commands to navigate your CDBs and their PDBs.

To connect to a pluggable database:

```
Filename: conn.sql
define pdb='&1'

ALTER SESSION SET CONTAINER=&pdb;
```
Usage: @conn.sql [PDB]

To determine the name of the PDB based on its GUID:

```
Filename: guid.sql
set lines 255 trims on
col name for a30
define guid='&1'
select name, dbid, con_id, con_uid , open_mode, total_size/1024/1024
total_size_mb,
block_size, proxy_pdb, local_undo
from v$pdbs
where guid='&guid'
/
```
Usage: @guid [GUID of the PDB]

Check on I/O activity for the past 1 minute:

```
Filename: io_mon_last_min.sql
set linesize 244 trims on
col pdb_name for a30
col begin_time for a30
col end_time for a30

alter session set nls_date_format='DD-MON-YYYY HH24:MI:SS';
alter session set nls_timestamp_format='DD-MON-YYYY HH24:MI:SS.FF';

SELECT c.con_id,
       c.pdb_name,
       r.begin_time,
       r.end_time,
       r.iops,
       r.iombps,
       r.iops_throttle_exempt,
       r.iombps_throttle_exempt,
       r.avg_io_throttle
FROM   v$rsrcpdbmetric r, cdb_pdbs c
WHERE  r.con_id =c.con_id
ORDER BY c.pdb_name;
```

Check on the I/O against PDBs for the past 1 hour:

```
Filename: io_mon_last_hour.sql
set linesize 244 trims on
col pdb_name for a30
col begin_time for a30
col end_time for a30

alter session set nls_date_format='DD-MON-YYYY HH24:MI:SS';
alter session set nls_timestamp_format='DD-MON-YYYY HH24:MI:SS.FF';
```

```
SELECT  c.con_id,
        c.pdb_name,
        r.begin_time,
        r.end_time,
        r.iops,
        r.iombps,
        r.iops_throttle_exempt,
        r.iombps_throttle_exempt,
        r.avg_io_throttle
FROM    v$rsrcpdbmetric_history r, cdb_pdbs c
WHERE   r.con_id = c.con_id
--AND    p.pdb_name = 'MyPDB'
ORDER BY r.begin_time;
```

Check on the I/O against historical information from the AWR repository:

```
Filename: io_mon_awr.sql
set linesize 244 trims on
col pdb_name for a30
col begin_time for a30
col end_time for a30

alter session set nls_date_format='DD-MON-YYYY HH24:MI:SS';
alter session set nls_timestamp_format='DD-MON-YYYY HH24:MI:SS.FF';

SELECT  r.snap_id,
        r.con_id,
        p.pdb_name,
        r.begin_time,
        r.end_time,
        r.iops,
        r.iombps,
        r.iops_throttle_exempt,
        r.iombps_throttle_exempt,
        r.avg_io_throttle
FROM    dba_hist_rsrc_pdb_metric r,
        cdb_pdbs p
WHERE   r.con_id = p.con_id
--AND    p.pdb_name = 'MyPDB'
ORDER BY r.begin_time;
```

Show the name and mode of each PDB:

```
Filename: pdbs.sql
set lines 122
col name for a50
SELECT con_id, name, open_mode FROM v$pdbs
/
```

Open a PDB in READ WRITE mode:

```
Filename: rw.sql
define pdb='&1'
ALTER PLUGGABLE DATABASE &pdb open;
```

PROD_AP Schema Population Scripts

The script to populate data into the **AP** schema of the **PROD_AP** PDB follows below.

```
/*
|| Script:  APInitialization.sql
|| Object:  Loads prototype Accounts Payable (AP) schema with test data
*/

-----
-- Deactivate constraints before table reloading
-----
ALTER TABLE ap.invoices
    DISABLE CONSTRAINT invoices_vendor_fk;
ALTER TABLE ap.invoice_items
    DISABLE CONSTRAINT invoice_items_invoice_fk;
TRUNCATE TABLE ap.invoice_items;
TRUNCATE TABLE ap.invoices;
TRUNCATE TABLE ap.vendors;


-----
-- Load test data into AP.VENDORS
-----
insert into AP.VENDORS (VENDOR_ID, ACTIVE_IND, NAME, ADDRESS_LINE_1, CITY, COUNTRY,
CREDIT_CARD, CREDIT_LIMIT)
values (101, 'Y', 'AT+T Corp.', '72 Firenze Street', 'Purley', 'United Kingdom',
'376434449021748', 513291);

insert into AP.VENDORS (VENDOR_ID, ACTIVE_IND, NAME, ADDRESS_LINE_1, CITY, STATE,
COUNTRY, CREDIT_CARD, CREDIT_LIMIT)
values (102, 'Y', 'Inspiration Software', '475 Dushku', 'Colorado Springs', 'CO', 'USA',
'372534433224561', 227134);

insert into AP.VENDORS (VENDOR_ID, ACTIVE_IND, NAME, ADDRESS_LINE_1, CITY, COUNTRY,
CREDIT_CARD, CREDIT_LIMIT)
values (103, 'Y', 'Data Company', '36 Herndon Road', 'Haverhill', 'United Kingdom',
'373334665723469', 415898);

insert into AP.VENDORS (VENDOR_ID, ACTIVE_IND, NAME, ADDRESS_LINE_1, CITY, COUNTRY,
CREDIT_CARD, CREDIT_LIMIT)
values (104, 'Y', 'Nestle', '573 Media Drive', 'Kanata', 'Canada', '378233947121626',
260424);

insert into AP.VENDORS (VENDOR_ID, ACTIVE_IND, NAME, ADDRESS_LINE_1, ADDRESS_LINE_2,
CITY, STATE, COUNTRY, CREDIT_CARD, CREDIT_LIMIT)
values (105, 'Y', 'Reckitt Benckiser', '10 Edmonton Blvd', 'Suite 100', 'Portland',
'ME', 'USA', '378433735921326', 432332);

insert into AP.VENDORS (VENDOR_ID, ACTIVE_IND, NAME, ADDRESS_LINE_1, CITY, STATE,
COUNTRY, CREDIT_CARD, CREDIT_LIMIT)
values (106, 'Y', 'Evergreen Resources', '80 Cesena Street', 'Carlsbad', 'CA', 'USA',
'373833403124834', 105077);

insert into AP.VENDORS (VENDOR_ID, ACTIVE_IND, NAME, ADDRESS_LINE_1, CITY, COUNTRY,
CREDIT_CARD, CREDIT_LIMIT)
values (107, 'Y', 'Questar Capital', '78 Reilly Street', 'Banbury', 'United Kingdom',
'376934280721694', 336060);

insert into AP.VENDORS (VENDOR_ID, ACTIVE_IND, NAME, ADDRESS_LINE_1, CITY, STATE,
COUNTRY, CREDIT_CARD, CREDIT_LIMIT)
values (108, 'Y', 'Conquest', '46 Dortmund Blvd', 'Delafield', 'WI', 'USA',
'375234655021950', 373989);

insert into AP.VENDORS (VENDOR_ID, ACTIVE_IND, NAME, ADDRESS_LINE_1, CITY, STATE,
COUNTRY, CREDIT_CARD, CREDIT_LIMIT)
values (109, 'Y', 'Learning Voyage', '69 Dunst Road', 'Mount Laurel', 'NJ', 'USA',
'378334289624106', 299626);

insert into AP.VENDORS (VENDOR_ID, ACTIVE_IND, NAME, ADDRESS_LINE_1, CITY, STATE,
COUNTRY, CREDIT_CARD, CREDIT_LIMIT)
values (110, 'Y', 'Connected', '76 Jackson Street', 'Waite Park', 'MN', 'USA',
'378833541521936', 716173);

insert into AP.VENDORS (VENDOR_ID, ACTIVE_IND, NAME, ADDRESS_LINE_1, CITY, COUNTRY,
CREDIT_CARD, CREDIT_LIMIT)
values (111, 'Y', 'Lynk Systems', '56 Phillippe', 'Tours', 'France', '377133513224568',
425335);

insert into AP.VENDORS (VENDOR_ID, ACTIVE_IND, NAME, ADDRESS_LINE_1, CITY, COUNTRY,
CREDIT_CARD, CREDIT_LIMIT)
```

```
values (112, 'Y', 'Yum Brands', '49 Gilberto Road', 'Sao caetano do sul', 'Brazil',
'378434349123812', 133840);

insert into AP.VENDORS (VENDOR_ID, ACTIVE_IND, NAME, ADDRESS_LINE_1, CITY, STATE,
COUNTRY, CREDIT_CARD, CREDIT_LIMIT)
values (113, 'Y', 'Oneida Financial', '33 Okayama Road', 'Research Triangle', 'NC',
'USA', '378933545924649', 252428);

insert into AP.VENDORS (VENDOR_ID, ACTIVE_IND, NAME, ADDRESS_LINE_1, CITY, COUNTRY,
CREDIT_CARD, CREDIT_LIMIT)
values (114, 'Y', 'Pyramid Digital Solutions', '98 Harriet Road', 'Ehningen', 'Germany',
'376133556123129', 690585);

insert into AP.VENDORS (VENDOR_ID, ACTIVE_IND, NAME, ADDRESS_LINE_1, CITY, COUNTRY,
CREDIT_CARD, CREDIT_LIMIT)
values (115, 'Y', 'Progressive Medical', '81 Celia', 'San Jose', 'Costa Rica',
'377534697124556', 684909);

insert into AP.VENDORS (VENDOR_ID, ACTIVE_IND, NAME, ADDRESS_LINE_1, CITY, COUNTRY,
CREDIT_CARD, CREDIT_LIMIT)
values (116, 'Y', 'American Pan and Engineering', '62nd Street', 'Verdun', 'Canada',
'378733697424451', 92827);

insert into AP.VENDORS (VENDOR_ID, ACTIVE_IND, NAME, ADDRESS_LINE_1, CITY, COUNTRY,
CREDIT_CARD, CREDIT_LIMIT)
values (117, 'Y', 'Unicru', '19 Capshaw Drive', 'Nagoya', 'Japan', '372733830424993',
317152);

insert into AP.VENDORS (VENDOR_ID, ACTIVE_IND, NAME, ADDRESS_LINE_1, CITY, COUNTRY,
CREDIT_CARD, CREDIT_LIMIT)
values (118, 'Y', 'ComGlobal Systems', '998 Bedelia Street', 'Pusan-city', 'South
Korea', '379534246521456', 135018);

insert into AP.VENDORS (VENDOR_ID, ACTIVE_IND, NAME, ADDRESS_LINE_1, CITY, STATE,
COUNTRY, CREDIT_CARD, CREDIT_LIMIT)
values (119, 'Y', 'Print-Tech', '51 Miles Street', 'Rochester', 'NY', 'USA',
'376634868722405', 59525);

insert into AP.VENDORS (VENDOR_ID, ACTIVE_IND, NAME, ADDRESS_LINE_1, CITY, COUNTRY,
CREDIT_CARD, CREDIT_LIMIT)
values (120, 'Y', 'Miller Systems', '62 Suvari Road', 'Mendoza', 'Argentina',
'375933896922553', 92369);

insert into AP.VENDORS (VENDOR_ID, ACTIVE_IND, NAME, ADDRESS_LINE_1, CITY, STATE,
COUNTRY, CREDIT_CARD, CREDIT_LIMIT)
values (121, 'Y', 'Intrasphere Technologies', '52 Durning Drive', 'Fort worth', 'TX',
'USA', '377133542224757', 108038);

insert into AP.VENDORS (VENDOR_ID, ACTIVE_IND, NAME, ADDRESS_LINE_1, CITY, STATE,
COUNTRY, CREDIT_CARD, CREDIT_LIMIT)
values (122, 'Y', 'Hencie', '3 Remar Road', 'Billerica', 'MA', 'USA', '377034903824533',
366566);

insert into AP.VENDORS (VENDOR_ID, ACTIVE_IND, NAME, ADDRESS_LINE_1, CITY, COUNTRY,
CREDIT_CARD, CREDIT_LIMIT)
values (123, 'Y', 'Urstadt Biddle Properties', '964 Pryce Street', 'Milton',
'Australia', '377034263722811', 525099);

insert into AP.VENDORS (VENDOR_ID, ACTIVE_IND, NAME, ADDRESS_LINE_1, CITY, STATE,
COUNTRY, CREDIT_CARD, CREDIT_LIMIT)
values (124, 'Y', 'Neogen', '83 Don Street', 'Flushing', 'NY', 'USA', '374333586923187',
454988);

insert into AP.VENDORS (VENDOR_ID, ACTIVE_IND, NAME, ADDRESS_LINE_1, CITY, COUNTRY,
CREDIT_CARD, CREDIT_LIMIT)
values (125, 'Y', 'Custom Solutions International', '85 Paltrow Road', 'Altstätten',
'Switzerland', '379533687021263', 307008);

insert into AP.VENDORS (VENDOR_ID, ACTIVE_IND, NAME, ADDRESS_LINE_1, CITY, COUNTRY,
CREDIT_CARD, CREDIT_LIMIT)
values (126, 'Y', 'Angie''s List', '28 Palminteri Ave', 'Kristiansand', 'Norway',
'374234482622480', 716259);

insert into AP.VENDORS (VENDOR_ID, ACTIVE_IND, NAME, ADDRESS_LINE_1, ADDRESS_LINE_2,
CITY, COUNTRY, CREDIT_CARD, CREDIT_LIMIT)
values (127, 'Y', 'Integrated Decisions and Systems', '86 Manu Ave', 'Building 10',
'Adelaide', 'Australia', '373634284023206', 440342);

insert into AP.VENDORS (VENDOR_ID, ACTIVE_IND, NAME, ADDRESS_LINE_1, CITY, COUNTRY,
CREDIT_CARD, CREDIT_LIMIT)
values (128, 'Y', 'Eastman Kodak Co.', '95 Page', 'Paris', 'France', '375934235623500',
372859);
```

```
insert into AP.VENDORS (VENDOR_ID, ACTIVE_IND, NAME, ADDRESS_LINE_1, CITY, COUNTRY,
CREDIT_CARD, CREDIT_LIMIT)
values (129, 'Y', 'Cold Stone Creamery', '918 Keith Street', 'Birmensdorf',
'Switzerland', '377134399823888', 583441);

insert into AP.VENDORS (VENDOR_ID, ACTIVE_IND, NAME, ADDRESS_LINE_1, CITY, STATE,
COUNTRY, CREDIT_CARD, CREDIT_LIMIT)
values (130, 'Y', 'Coadvantage Resources', '23rd Street', 'Media', 'PA', 'USA',
'374234357323177', 411822);

insert into AP.VENDORS (VENDOR_ID, ACTIVE_IND, NAME, ADDRESS_LINE_1, CITY, COUNTRY,
CREDIT_CARD, CREDIT_LIMIT)
values (131, 'Y', 'Cowlitz Bancorp', '83 Cumming Road', 'São paulo', 'Brazil',
'373534847324051', 643506);

insert into AP.VENDORS (VENDOR_ID, ACTIVE_IND, NAME, ADDRESS_LINE_1, CITY, COUNTRY,
CREDIT_CARD, CREDIT_LIMIT)
values (132, 'Y', 'Coca-Cola Co.', '49 Uggams Road', 'Itu', 'Brazil', '373934061222025',
738605);

insert into AP.VENDORS (VENDOR_ID, ACTIVE_IND, NAME, ADDRESS_LINE_1, CITY, COUNTRY,
CREDIT_CARD, CREDIT_LIMIT)
values (133, 'Y', 'Black Mountain Management', '56 Benjamin', 'Wellington', 'New
Zealand', '374633169824561', 195004);

insert into AP.VENDORS (VENDOR_ID, ACTIVE_IND, NAME, ADDRESS_LINE_1, CITY, COUNTRY,
CREDIT_CARD, CREDIT_LIMIT)
values (134, 'Y', 'Schering-Plough Corp.', '6 Olyphant Ave', 'Tbilisi', 'Georgia',
'377433987522529', 75500);

insert into AP.VENDORS (VENDOR_ID, ACTIVE_IND, NAME, ADDRESS_LINE_1, CITY, COUNTRY,
CREDIT_CARD, CREDIT_LIMIT)
values (135, 'Y', 'Walt Disney Co.', '26 Pusan Street', 'Helsingborg', 'Sweden',
'375934025921083', 200700);

insert into AP.VENDORS (VENDOR_ID, ACTIVE_IND, NAME, ADDRESS_LINE_1, CITY, STATE,
COUNTRY, CREDIT_CARD, CREDIT_LIMIT)
values (136, 'Y', 'Wells Financial', '30 Sharp Street', 'Orlando', 'FL', 'USA',
'377034135722429', 553776);

insert into AP.VENDORS (VENDOR_ID, ACTIVE_IND, NAME, ADDRESS_LINE_1, CITY, STATE,
COUNTRY, CREDIT_CARD, CREDIT_LIMIT)
values (137, 'Y', 'Palm Beach Tan', '16 Berry Street', 'Hunt Valley', 'MD', 'USA',
'376734267322743', 746050);

insert into AP.VENDORS (VENDOR_ID, ACTIVE_IND, NAME, ADDRESS_LINE_1, CITY, STATE,
COUNTRY, CREDIT_CARD, CREDIT_LIMIT)
values (138, 'Y', 'J.C. Penney Corp.', '39 Osment Drive', 'Bradenton', 'FL', 'USA',
'379433356522360', 320232);

insert into AP.VENDORS (VENDOR_ID, ACTIVE_IND, NAME, ADDRESS_LINE_1, CITY, STATE,
COUNTRY, CREDIT_CARD, CREDIT_LIMIT)
values (139, 'Y', 'Urstadt Biddle Properties', '90 Heiligenhaus', 'Sugar Hill', 'GA',
'USA', '379533500921109', 588562);

insert into AP.VENDORS (VENDOR_ID, ACTIVE_IND, NAME, ADDRESS_LINE_1, CITY, STATE,
COUNTRY, CREDIT_CARD, CREDIT_LIMIT)
values (140, 'Y', 'Flow Management Technologies', '56 Joshua', 'Concordville', 'PA',
'USA', '373933866621140', 660472);

insert into AP.VENDORS (VENDOR_ID, ACTIVE_IND, NAME, ADDRESS_LINE_1, CITY, STATE,
COUNTRY, CREDIT_CARD, CREDIT_LIMIT)
values (141, 'Y', 'Prosperity Bancshares', '12 Freddie Road', 'Lehi', 'UT', 'USA',
'373134873122933', 368206);

insert into AP.VENDORS (VENDOR_ID, ACTIVE_IND, NAME, ADDRESS_LINE_1, CITY, COUNTRY,
CREDIT_CARD, CREDIT_LIMIT)
values (142, 'Y', '3t Systems', '178 Madeleine Drive', 'Grand-mere', 'Canada',
'378034130324085', 442068);

insert into AP.VENDORS (VENDOR_ID, ACTIVE_IND, NAME, ADDRESS_LINE_1, CITY, COUNTRY,
CREDIT_CARD, CREDIT_LIMIT)
values (143, 'Y', 'Caliber Collision Centers', '4 Boyle Road', 'Chiba', 'Japan',
'379534841721190', 440432);

insert into AP.VENDORS (VENDOR_ID, ACTIVE_IND, NAME, ADDRESS_LINE_1, CITY, STATE,
COUNTRY, CREDIT_CARD, CREDIT_LIMIT)
values (144, 'Y', 'Bio-Reference Labs', '91 Berry Street', 'Fairview Heights', 'IL',
'USA', '377833515823872', 214866);

insert into AP.VENDORS (VENDOR_ID, ACTIVE_IND, NAME, ADDRESS_LINE_1, CITY, COUNTRY,
CREDIT_CARD, CREDIT_LIMIT)
```

```sql
values (145, 'Y', 'Cima Consulting Group', '30 Rhames Road', 'Frankfurt am Main',
'Germany', '380134428223569', 304220);

insert into AP.VENDORS (VENDOR_ID, ACTIVE_IND, NAME, ADDRESS_LINE_1, CITY, STATE,
COUNTRY, CREDIT_CARD, CREDIT_LIMIT)
values (146, 'Y', 'Phoenix Rehabilitation and Health Services', '21 Ty Street',
'Salisbury', 'NC', 'USA', '379234184621620', 612978);

insert into AP.VENDORS (VENDOR_ID, ACTIVE_IND, NAME, ADDRESS_LINE_1, CITY, STATE,
COUNTRY, CREDIT_CARD, CREDIT_LIMIT)
values (147, 'Y', 'EPIQ Systems', '35 Cassel', 'Brentwood', 'TN', 'USA',
'375534694622968', 727296);

insert into AP.VENDORS (VENDOR_ID, ACTIVE_IND, NAME, ADDRESS_LINE_1, CITY, COUNTRY,
CREDIT_CARD, CREDIT_LIMIT)
values (148, 'Y', 'IBM Corp.', '1 Trick Street', 'Soest', 'Netherlands',
'378734444424972', 130674);

insert into AP.VENDORS (VENDOR_ID, ACTIVE_IND, NAME, ADDRESS_LINE_1, ADDRESS_LINE_2,
CITY, COUNTRY, CREDIT_CARD, CREDIT_LIMIT)
values (149, 'Y', 'Advanced Vision Research', '83 Boothe', 'Suite 200', 'West
Launceston', 'Australia', '376233927622489', 41544);

insert into AP.VENDORS (VENDOR_ID, ACTIVE_IND, NAME, ADDRESS_LINE_1, CITY, COUNTRY,
CREDIT_CARD, CREDIT_LIMIT)
values (150, 'Y', 'Lindin Consulting', '56 Bingham Farms Road', 'Anyang-si', 'South
Korea', '377833138223331', 525405);

insert into AP.VENDORS (VENDOR_ID, ACTIVE_IND, NAME, ADDRESS_LINE_1, ADDRESS_LINE_2,
CITY, COUNTRY, CREDIT_CARD, CREDIT_LIMIT)
values (151, 'Y', 'Comnet International', '24 Englund Road', 'Suite 200', 'Belgrad',
'Yugoslavia', '376434228023022', 176094);

insert into AP.VENDORS (VENDOR_ID, ACTIVE_IND, NAME, ADDRESS_LINE_1, CITY, COUNTRY,
CREDIT_CARD, CREDIT_LIMIT)
values (152, 'Y', 'Tripwire', '47 Darren', 'Almaty', 'Kazakstan', '377534921821984',
253301);

insert into AP.VENDORS (VENDOR_ID, ACTIVE_IND, NAME, ADDRESS_LINE_1, CITY, COUNTRY,
CREDIT_CARD, CREDIT_LIMIT)
values (153, 'Y', 'SafeHome Security', '38 Jonny Lee Drive', 'Birmingham', 'United
Kingdom', '375634403521629', 621063);

insert into AP.VENDORS (VENDOR_ID, ACTIVE_IND, NAME, ADDRESS_LINE_1, CITY, COUNTRY,
CREDIT_CARD, CREDIT_LIMIT)
values (154, 'Y', 'E Group', '32 Rhea Road', 'Rothenburg', 'Germany', '376133826421299',
549687);

insert into AP.VENDORS (VENDOR_ID, ACTIVE_IND, NAME, ADDRESS_LINE_1, CITY, COUNTRY,
CREDIT_CARD, CREDIT_LIMIT)
values (155, 'Y', 'Direct Data', '8 Debra Road', 'Milano', 'Italy', '374634948421795',
446638);

insert into AP.VENDORS (VENDOR_ID, ACTIVE_IND, NAME, ADDRESS_LINE_1, CITY, COUNTRY,
CREDIT_CARD, CREDIT_LIMIT)
values (156, 'Y', 'GTS Refreshment Services', '31 Goteborg Road', 'Sursee',
'Switzerland', '375834911221414', 447548);

insert into AP.VENDORS (VENDOR_ID, ACTIVE_IND, NAME, ADDRESS_LINE_1, CITY, COUNTRY,
CREDIT_CARD, CREDIT_LIMIT)
values (157, 'Y', 'Educational Development', '82 Hatfield Street', 'Manaus', 'Brazil',
'372733486423570', 557688);

insert into AP.VENDORS (VENDOR_ID, ACTIVE_IND, NAME, ADDRESS_LINE_1, CITY, COUNTRY,
CREDIT_CARD, CREDIT_LIMIT)
values (158, 'Y', 'America''s Choice Healthplans', '87 Voight Road', 'Nara', 'Japan',
'375834343221582', 388628);

insert into AP.VENDORS (VENDOR_ID, ACTIVE_IND, NAME, ADDRESS_LINE_1, CITY, COUNTRY,
CREDIT_CARD, CREDIT_LIMIT)
values (159, 'Y', 'Visionary Systems', '72 Perez Road', 'Colombes', 'France',
'374234188621332', 630498);

insert into AP.VENDORS (VENDOR_ID, ACTIVE_IND, NAME, ADDRESS_LINE_1, CITY, COUNTRY,
CREDIT_CARD, CREDIT_LIMIT)
values (160, 'Y', 'Partnership in Building', '23 Bryson Drive', 'Tilst', 'Denmark',
'379834042322458', 435859);

insert into AP.VENDORS (VENDOR_ID, ACTIVE_IND, NAME, ADDRESS_LINE_1, CITY, COUNTRY,
CREDIT_CARD, CREDIT_LIMIT)
values (161, 'Y', 'FFLC Bancorp', '565 Gershon Road', 'Steyr', 'Austria',
'375333375922692', 304084);
```

```sql
insert into AP.VENDORS (VENDOR_ID, ACTIVE_IND, NAME, ADDRESS_LINE_1, CITY, COUNTRY,
CREDIT_CARD, CREDIT_LIMIT)
values (162, 'Y', 'Staff Force', '69 Rich Drive', 'Sant Cugat Del Valle', 'Spain',
'372433800524925', 296871);

insert into AP.VENDORS (VENDOR_ID, ACTIVE_IND, NAME, ADDRESS_LINE_1, CITY, STATE,
COUNTRY, CREDIT_CARD, CREDIT_LIMIT)
values (163, 'Y', 'Gap Inc.', '944 Hannah Street', 'Mclean', 'VA', 'USA',
'373734939422108', 736384);

insert into AP.VENDORS (VENDOR_ID, ACTIVE_IND, NAME, ADDRESS_LINE_1, CITY, COUNTRY,
CREDIT_CARD, CREDIT_LIMIT)
values (164, 'Y', 'Serentec', '46 McNeice Ave', 'Milsons Point', 'Australia',
'377834675824016', 615414);

insert into AP.VENDORS (VENDOR_ID, ACTIVE_IND, NAME, ADDRESS_LINE_1, CITY, STATE,
COUNTRY, CREDIT_CARD, CREDIT_LIMIT)
values (165, 'Y', 'StoneTech Professional', '51 Santa Cruz Road', 'Portland', 'ME',
'USA', '375234777922198', 400769);

insert into AP.VENDORS (VENDOR_ID, ACTIVE_IND, NAME, ADDRESS_LINE_1, ADDRESS_LINE_2,
CITY, COUNTRY, CREDIT_CARD, CREDIT_LIMIT)
values (166, 'Y', 'Staff Force', '51st Street', 'Building 10', 'Ipswich', 'United
Kingdom', '378633508922043', 410911);

insert into AP.VENDORS (VENDOR_ID, ACTIVE_IND, NAME, ADDRESS_LINE_1, CITY, COUNTRY,
CREDIT_CARD, CREDIT_LIMIT)
values (167, 'Y', 'ZonePerfect Nutrition Company', '62nd Street', 'Wehrheim', 'Germany',
'379233670021049', 125907);

insert into AP.VENDORS (VENDOR_ID, ACTIVE_IND, NAME, ADDRESS_LINE_1, ADDRESS_LINE_2,
CITY, STATE, COUNTRY, CREDIT_CARD, CREDIT_LIMIT)
values (168, 'Y', 'Prosoft Technology Group', '47 Lake Forest', 'Suite 101',
'Salisbury', 'NC', 'USA', '374933361522953', 459642);

insert into AP.VENDORS (VENDOR_ID, ACTIVE_IND, NAME, ADDRESS_LINE_1, CITY, COUNTRY,
CREDIT_CARD, CREDIT_LIMIT)
values (169, 'Y', 'May Department Stores Co.', '56 Vince Road', 'Echirolles', 'France',
'379234564121140', 247483);

insert into AP.VENDORS (VENDOR_ID, ACTIVE_IND, NAME, ADDRESS_LINE_1, CITY, STATE,
COUNTRY, CREDIT_CARD, CREDIT_LIMIT)
values (170, 'Y', 'Solipsys', '97 Whitford Blvd', 'Charleston', 'TN', 'USA',
'376333323521841', 336905);

insert into AP.VENDORS (VENDOR_ID, ACTIVE_IND, NAME, ADDRESS_LINE_1, CITY, COUNTRY,
CREDIT_CARD, CREDIT_LIMIT)
values (171, 'Y', 'Turner Professional Services', '60 Carlin Road', 'Vilafranca
Penedes', 'Spain', '377933659623671', 85428);

insert into AP.VENDORS (VENDOR_ID, ACTIVE_IND, NAME, ADDRESS_LINE_1, CITY, COUNTRY,
CREDIT_CARD, CREDIT_LIMIT)
values (172, 'Y', 'Diamond Group', '651 El Segundo Drive', 'Paço de Arcos', 'Portugal',
'373134471424236', 445827);

insert into AP.VENDORS (VENDOR_ID, ACTIVE_IND, NAME, ADDRESS_LINE_1, CITY, STATE,
COUNTRY, CREDIT_CARD, CREDIT_LIMIT)
values (173, 'Y', 'Montpelier Plastics', '30 Lisbon Drive', 'California', 'MD', 'USA',
'378833532722472', 115500);

insert into AP.VENDORS (VENDOR_ID, ACTIVE_IND, NAME, ADDRESS_LINE_1, CITY, COUNTRY,
CREDIT_CARD, CREDIT_LIMIT)
values (174, 'Y', 'Tilson Landscape', '9 Taryn Drive', 'Utrecht', 'Netherlands',
'379934270623147', 27385);

insert into AP.VENDORS (VENDOR_ID, ACTIVE_IND, NAME, ADDRESS_LINE_1, CITY, COUNTRY,
CREDIT_CARD, CREDIT_LIMIT)
values (175, 'Y', 'Elite Computers and Software', '11 Voight Blvd', 'Mito', 'Japan',
'375833977924705', 136434);

insert into AP.VENDORS (VENDOR_ID, ACTIVE_IND, NAME, ADDRESS_LINE_1, CITY, COUNTRY,
CREDIT_CARD, CREDIT_LIMIT)
values (176, 'Y', 'Wal-Mart Stores', '30 Liv Street', 'Suwon-city', 'South Korea',
'376333115723807', 82000);

insert into AP.VENDORS (VENDOR_ID, ACTIVE_IND, NAME, ADDRESS_LINE_1, CITY, COUNTRY,
CREDIT_CARD, CREDIT_LIMIT)
values (177, 'Y', 'MidAmerica Auto Glass', '39 Fiennes Street', 'Brossard', 'Canada',
'375333466523234', 584569);

insert into AP.VENDORS (VENDOR_ID, ACTIVE_IND, NAME, ADDRESS_LINE_1, CITY, COUNTRY,
CREDIT_CARD, CREDIT_LIMIT)
```

```sql
values (178, 'Y', 'ORI Services', '261 Bragg Drive', 'Newton-le-willows', 'United
Kingdom', '377733573422346', 452988);

insert into AP.VENDORS (VENDOR_ID, ACTIVE_IND, NAME, ADDRESS_LINE_1, CITY, STATE,
COUNTRY, CREDIT_CARD, CREDIT_LIMIT)
values (179, 'Y', 'Authoria', '100 Cesena Ave', 'Springville', 'CA', 'USA',
'373733173223516', 130373);

insert into AP.VENDORS (VENDOR_ID, ACTIVE_IND, NAME, ADDRESS_LINE_1, CITY, COUNTRY,
CREDIT_CARD, CREDIT_LIMIT)
values (180, 'Y', 'Grant Harrison Advertising', '68 Neil Road', 'Ankara', 'Turkey',
'377934357721870', 701039);

insert into AP.VENDORS (VENDOR_ID, ACTIVE_IND, NAME, ADDRESS_LINE_1, CITY, COUNTRY,
CREDIT_CARD, CREDIT_LIMIT)
values (181, 'Y', 'Cody-Kramer Imports', '68 Richie Ave', 'Joinville', 'Brazil',
'377634001921656', 444972);

insert into AP.VENDORS (VENDOR_ID, ACTIVE_IND, NAME, ADDRESS_LINE_1, CITY, COUNTRY,
CREDIT_CARD, CREDIT_LIMIT)
values (182, 'Y', 'Coridian Technologies', '95 Wincott Blvd', 'Valencia', 'Spain',
'380033930823978', 210494);

insert into AP.VENDORS (VENDOR_ID, ACTIVE_IND, NAME, ADDRESS_LINE_1, CITY, COUNTRY,
CREDIT_CARD, CREDIT_LIMIT)
values (183, 'Y', 'Prometheus Laboratories', '927 Colm Street', 'Birmensdorf',
'Switzerland', '373034599422004', 358256);

insert into AP.VENDORS (VENDOR_ID, ACTIVE_IND, NAME, ADDRESS_LINE_1, CITY, COUNTRY,
CREDIT_CARD, CREDIT_LIMIT)
values (184, 'Y', 'Peerless Manufacturing', '84 Solido Road', 'Burlington', 'Canada',
'375934161621529', 302335);

insert into AP.VENDORS (VENDOR_ID, ACTIVE_IND, NAME, ADDRESS_LINE_1, CITY, COUNTRY,
CREDIT_CARD, CREDIT_LIMIT)
values (185, 'Y', 'Global Science and Technology', '272 Harriet', 'Hiroshima', 'Japan',
'375434074824297', 140505);

insert into AP.VENDORS (VENDOR_ID, ACTIVE_IND, NAME, ADDRESS_LINE_1, ADDRESS_LINE_2,
CITY, COUNTRY, CREDIT_CARD, CREDIT_LIMIT)
values (186, 'Y', 'Business Plus Corporation', '73 Knutsford Ave', 'Building 10', 'Itu',
'Brazil', '379834931922245', 340773);

insert into AP.VENDORS (VENDOR_ID, ACTIVE_IND, NAME, ADDRESS_LINE_1, CITY, COUNTRY,
CREDIT_CARD, CREDIT_LIMIT)
values (187, 'Y', 'Market-Based Solutions', '74 Bruxelles', 'Ankara', 'Turkey',
'379833392921341', 690599);

insert into AP.VENDORS (VENDOR_ID, ACTIVE_IND, NAME, ADDRESS_LINE_1, CITY, COUNTRY,
CREDIT_CARD, CREDIT_LIMIT)
values (188, 'Y', 'Vertex Solutions', '571 Loveless Drive', 'Tartu', 'Estonia',
'375534469621175', 667940);

insert into AP.VENDORS (VENDOR_ID, ACTIVE_IND, NAME, ADDRESS_LINE_1, CITY, COUNTRY,
CREDIT_CARD, CREDIT_LIMIT)
values (189, 'Y', 'Gold Crest Distributing', '445 Guy Ave', 'Solikamsk', 'Russia',
'374733521123943', 130572);

insert into AP.VENDORS (VENDOR_ID, ACTIVE_IND, NAME, ADDRESS_LINE_1, CITY, COUNTRY,
CREDIT_CARD, CREDIT_LIMIT)
values (190, 'Y', 'American Service Systems', '99 Akita Street', 'Drogenbos', 'Belgium',
'377433226724224', 303642);

insert into AP.VENDORS (VENDOR_ID, ACTIVE_IND, NAME, ADDRESS_LINE_1, CITY, COUNTRY,
CREDIT_CARD, CREDIT_LIMIT)
values (191, 'Y', 'Strategic Management Initiatives', '33 Juno Beach Ave', 'Ringwood',
'Australia', '372834347523532', 327204);

insert into AP.VENDORS (VENDOR_ID, ACTIVE_IND, NAME, ADDRESS_LINE_1, CITY, COUNTRY,
CREDIT_CARD, CREDIT_LIMIT)
values (192, 'Y', 'Liners Direct', '850 Connie', 'St Leonards', 'Australia',
'377634440724486', 744767);

insert into AP.VENDORS (VENDOR_ID, ACTIVE_IND, NAME, ADDRESS_LINE_1, CITY, STATE,
COUNTRY, CREDIT_CARD, CREDIT_LIMIT)
values (193, 'Y', 'Sandy Spring Bancorp', '82 Geneva Street', 'Sarasota', 'FL', 'USA',
'378934635822435', 665999);

insert into AP.VENDORS (VENDOR_ID, ACTIVE_IND, NAME, ADDRESS_LINE_1, CITY, STATE,
COUNTRY, CREDIT_CARD, CREDIT_LIMIT)
values (194, 'Y', 'RS Information Systems', '68 Liam Drive', 'Lake Forest', 'CA', 'USA',
'374133871321694', 567911);
```

```
insert into AP.VENDORS (VENDOR_ID, ACTIVE_IND, NAME, ADDRESS_LINE_1, CITY, COUNTRY,
CREDIT_CARD, CREDIT_LIMIT)
values (195, 'Y', 'Evinco', '92nd Street', 'Radovljica', 'Slovenia', '379733108123566',
719943);

insert into AP.VENDORS (VENDOR_ID, ACTIVE_IND, NAME, ADDRESS_LINE_1, CITY, STATE,
COUNTRY, CREDIT_CARD, CREDIT_LIMIT)
values (196, 'Y', 'ScriptSave', '8 Goran Ave', 'North bethesda', 'MD', 'USA',
'373734689624935', 419899);

insert into AP.VENDORS (VENDOR_ID, ACTIVE_IND, NAME, ADDRESS_LINE_1, CITY, COUNTRY,
CREDIT_CARD, CREDIT_LIMIT)
values (197, 'Y', 'Synhrgy HR Technologies', '23rd Street', 'Brossard', 'Canada',
'380134491824399', 335130);

insert into AP.VENDORS (VENDOR_ID, ACTIVE_IND, NAME, ADDRESS_LINE_1, CITY, COUNTRY,
CREDIT_CARD, CREDIT_LIMIT)
values (198, 'Y', 'Unicru', '481 Botti Street', 'Eiksmarka', 'Norway',
'376333204523112', 549994);

insert into AP.VENDORS (VENDOR_ID, ACTIVE_IND, NAME, ADDRESS_LINE_1, CITY, COUNTRY,
CREDIT_CARD, CREDIT_LIMIT)
values (199, 'Y', 'Cima Labs', '903 Hoskins Drive', 'Nagoya', 'Japan',
'372534371722151', 713949);

insert into AP.VENDORS (VENDOR_ID, ACTIVE_IND, NAME, ADDRESS_LINE_1, CITY, COUNTRY,
CREDIT_CARD, CREDIT_LIMIT)
values (200, 'Y', 'SSCI', '8 Bette Ave', 'Rotterdam', 'Netherlands', '379334912821474',
705724);

insert into AP.VENDORS (VENDOR_ID, ACTIVE_IND, NAME, ADDRESS_LINE_1, CITY, STATE,
COUNTRY, CREDIT_CARD, CREDIT_LIMIT)
values (201, 'Y', 'Hospital Solutions', '23 Kurtz Blvd', 'O''fallon', 'IL', 'USA',
'376834310723899', 593658);

insert into AP.VENDORS (VENDOR_ID, ACTIVE_IND, NAME, ADDRESS_LINE_1, CITY, COUNTRY,
CREDIT_CARD, CREDIT_LIMIT)
values (202, 'Y', 'Telechem International', '793 Rossellini Street', 'Mendoza',
'Argentina', '380034345924810', 108495);

insert into AP.VENDORS (VENDOR_ID, ACTIVE_IND, NAME, ADDRESS_LINE_1, CITY, STATE,
COUNTRY, CREDIT_CARD, CREDIT_LIMIT)
values (203, 'Y', 'Veri-Tek International', '91st Street', 'Nashua', 'NH', 'USA',
'379234922523349', 162621);

insert into AP.VENDORS (VENDOR_ID, ACTIVE_IND, NAME, ADDRESS_LINE_1, CITY, COUNTRY,
CREDIT_CARD, CREDIT_LIMIT)
values (204, 'Y', 'Parksite', '895 Unger Street', 'Dortmund', 'Germany',
'373433849124542', 362673);

insert into AP.VENDORS (VENDOR_ID, ACTIVE_IND, NAME, ADDRESS_LINE_1, CITY, STATE,
COUNTRY, CREDIT_CARD, CREDIT_LIMIT)
values (205, 'Y', 'Genghis Grill', '278 Mykelti Road', 'Los Angeles', 'CA', 'USA',
'377533831321447', 636419);

insert into AP.VENDORS (VENDOR_ID, ACTIVE_IND, NAME, ADDRESS_LINE_1, CITY, STATE,
COUNTRY, CREDIT_CARD, CREDIT_LIMIT)
values (206, 'Y', 'Imports By Four Hands', '95 Marina Street', 'Lathrop', 'CA', 'USA',
'375533694824328', 729281);

insert into AP.VENDORS (VENDOR_ID, ACTIVE_IND, NAME, ADDRESS_LINE_1, CITY, COUNTRY,
CREDIT_CARD, CREDIT_LIMIT)
values (207, 'Y', 'Extra Mile Transportation', '34 Macclesfield Blvd', 'Ebersberg',
'Germany', '374433557223728', 386344);

insert into AP.VENDORS (VENDOR_ID, ACTIVE_IND, NAME, ADDRESS_LINE_1, CITY, COUNTRY,
CREDIT_CARD, CREDIT_LIMIT)
values (208, 'Y', 'Greenwich Technology Partners', '56 Balin Street', 'Durban', 'South
Africa', '375334634224722', 260007);

insert into AP.VENDORS (VENDOR_ID, ACTIVE_IND, NAME, ADDRESS_LINE_1, CITY, COUNTRY,
CREDIT_CARD, CREDIT_LIMIT)
values (209, 'Y', 'Arkidata', '88 Rodgers Road', 'Storrington', 'United Kingdom',
'376333637921832', 670179);

insert into AP.VENDORS (VENDOR_ID, ACTIVE_IND, NAME, ADDRESS_LINE_1, CITY, STATE,
COUNTRY, CREDIT_CARD, CREDIT_LIMIT)
values (210, 'Y', 'Kia Motors Corp.', '11 Clarence Blvd', 'Newnan', 'GA', 'USA',
'374233687923382', 565650);

insert into AP.VENDORS (VENDOR_ID, ACTIVE_IND, NAME, ADDRESS_LINE_1, CITY, COUNTRY,
CREDIT_CARD, CREDIT_LIMIT)
```

```
values (211, 'Y', 'Mission West Properties', '34 Reiner Street', 'Manaus', 'Brazil',
'377334547321543', 302236);

insert into AP.VENDORS (VENDOR_ID, ACTIVE_IND, NAME, ADDRESS_LINE_1, CITY, COUNTRY,
CREDIT_CARD, CREDIT_LIMIT)
values (212, 'Y', 'Toyota Motor Corp.', '15 Geoffrey Road', 'Cesena', 'Italy',
'376634956921266', 343546);

insert into AP.VENDORS (VENDOR_ID, ACTIVE_IND, NAME, ADDRESS_LINE_1, CITY, COUNTRY,
CREDIT_CARD, CREDIT_LIMIT)
values (213, 'Y', 'Black Mountain Management', '55 DiCaprio Blvd', 'Bracknell', 'United
Kingdom', '375533342922873', 93576);

insert into AP.VENDORS (VENDOR_ID, ACTIVE_IND, NAME, ADDRESS_LINE_1, CITY, COUNTRY,
CREDIT_CARD, CREDIT_LIMIT)
values (214, 'Y', 'U.S. Government', '50 Thomas Street', 'Fuerth', 'Germany',
'376134251323234', 473014);

insert into AP.VENDORS (VENDOR_ID, ACTIVE_IND, NAME, ADDRESS_LINE_1, CITY, STATE,
COUNTRY, CREDIT_CARD, CREDIT_LIMIT)
values (215, 'Y', 'Pacific Data Designs', '8 Nicolas Street', 'Stoneham', 'MA', 'USA',
'375334721422833', 335833);

insert into AP.VENDORS (VENDOR_ID, ACTIVE_IND, NAME, ADDRESS_LINE_1, CITY, STATE,
COUNTRY, CREDIT_CARD, CREDIT_LIMIT)
values (216, 'Y', 'Miller Systems', '1 Raybon Street', 'Bingham Farms', 'MI', 'USA',
'375133398023251', 620689);

insert into AP.VENDORS (VENDOR_ID, ACTIVE_IND, NAME, ADDRESS_LINE_1, CITY, COUNTRY,
CREDIT_CARD, CREDIT_LIMIT)
values (217, 'Y', 'Carteret Mortgage', '91st Street', 'Münster', 'Germany',
'378034684624050', 100627);

insert into AP.VENDORS (VENDOR_ID, ACTIVE_IND, NAME, ADDRESS_LINE_1, ADDRESS_LINE_2,
CITY, COUNTRY, CREDIT_CARD, CREDIT_LIMIT)
values (218, 'Y', 'American Vanguard', '6 Gloria Road', 'Suite 101', 'Alleroed',
'Denmark', '378834720222697', 116168);

insert into AP.VENDORS (VENDOR_ID, ACTIVE_IND, NAME, ADDRESS_LINE_1, CITY, STATE,
COUNTRY, CREDIT_CARD, CREDIT_LIMIT)
values (219, 'Y', 'ACS International Resources', '9 Lang Road', 'Key Biscayne', 'FL',
'USA', '379633560922588', 369185);

insert into AP.VENDORS (VENDOR_ID, ACTIVE_IND, NAME, ADDRESS_LINE_1, CITY, STATE,
COUNTRY, CREDIT_CARD, CREDIT_LIMIT)
values (220, 'Y', 'Glacier Bancorp', '87 Marietta Ave', 'Murray', 'UT', 'USA',
'376734378521339', 393308);

insert into AP.VENDORS (VENDOR_ID, ACTIVE_IND, NAME, ADDRESS_LINE_1, CITY, STATE,
COUNTRY, CREDIT_CARD, CREDIT_LIMIT)
values (221, 'Y', 'White Wave', '4 Ellis Ave', 'Streamwood', 'IL', 'USA',
'373634985321920', 492928);

insert into AP.VENDORS (VENDOR_ID, ACTIVE_IND, NAME, ADDRESS_LINE_1, ADDRESS_LINE_2,
CITY, STATE, COUNTRY, CREDIT_CARD, CREDIT_LIMIT)
values (222, 'Y', 'Quicksilver Resources', '32 Elkins Park Blvd', 'Suite 200', 'Santa
Clarita', 'CA', 'USA', '374934202822119', 692663);

insert into AP.VENDORS (VENDOR_ID, ACTIVE_IND, NAME, ADDRESS_LINE_1, ADDRESS_LINE_2,
CITY, COUNTRY, CREDIT_CARD, CREDIT_LIMIT)
values (223, 'Y', 'Astute', '78 Curt Road', 'Office 99', 'Holderbank', 'Switzerland',
'376533395624214', 171133);

insert into AP.VENDORS (VENDOR_ID, ACTIVE_IND, NAME, ADDRESS_LINE_1, ADDRESS_LINE_2,
CITY, STATE, COUNTRY, CREDIT_CARD, CREDIT_LIMIT)
values (224, 'Y', 'Keller Williams Realty Ahwatukee Foothills', '33 Zahn Ave', 'Suite
100', 'Farmington Hills', 'MI', 'USA', '379234547623754', 375241);

insert into AP.VENDORS (VENDOR_ID, ACTIVE_IND, NAME, ADDRESS_LINE_1, CITY, STATE,
COUNTRY, CREDIT_CARD, CREDIT_LIMIT)
values (225, 'Y', 'WCI', '63rd Street', 'San Francisco', 'CA', 'USA', '372633433723143',
426351);

insert into AP.VENDORS (VENDOR_ID, ACTIVE_IND, NAME, ADDRESS_LINE_1, CITY, COUNTRY,
CREDIT_CARD, CREDIT_LIMIT)
values (226, 'Y', 'Caliber Collision Centers', '8 North Point Road', 'Summerside',
'Canada', '379134740124231', 235174);

insert into AP.VENDORS (VENDOR_ID, ACTIVE_IND, NAME, ADDRESS_LINE_1, CITY, STATE,
COUNTRY, CREDIT_CARD, CREDIT_LIMIT)
values (227, 'Y', 'FirstFed America Bancorp', '11 Sulzbach Road', 'Salisbury', 'NC',
'USA', '375734080523615', 398629);
```

```
insert into AP.VENDORS (VENDOR_ID, ACTIVE_IND, NAME, ADDRESS_LINE_1, CITY, STATE,
COUNTRY, CREDIT_CARD, CREDIT_LIMIT)
values (228, 'Y', 'Intrasphere Technologies', '13rd Street', 'Caguas', 'PR', 'USA',
'376433252721861', 666044);

insert into AP.VENDORS (VENDOR_ID, ACTIVE_IND, NAME, ADDRESS_LINE_1, CITY, STATE,
COUNTRY, CREDIT_CARD, CREDIT_LIMIT)
values (229, 'Y', 'First South Bancorp', '904 Fountain Hills Ave', 'Blacksburg', 'VA',
'USA', '379634387223137', 337420);

insert into AP.VENDORS (VENDOR_ID, ACTIVE_IND, NAME, ADDRESS_LINE_1, CITY, COUNTRY,
CREDIT_CARD, CREDIT_LIMIT)
values (230, 'Y', 'SEI/Aaron''s', '62nd Street', 'Nordhausen', 'Germany',
'376434836723520', 173674);

insert into AP.VENDORS (VENDOR_ID, ACTIVE_IND, NAME, ADDRESS_LINE_1, ADDRESS_LINE_2,
CITY, COUNTRY, CREDIT_CARD, CREDIT_LIMIT)
values (231, 'Y', 'Denali Ventures', '99 Maura Street', 'Suite 200', 'Kloten',
'Switzerland', '377233734222434', 184279);

insert into AP.VENDORS (VENDOR_ID, ACTIVE_IND, NAME, ADDRESS_LINE_1, CITY, STATE,
COUNTRY, CREDIT_CARD, CREDIT_LIMIT)
values (232, 'Y', 'Capital Crossing Bank', '11 Eliza Road', 'Santa Clarita', 'CA',
'USA', '377133334321285', 488030);

insert into AP.VENDORS (VENDOR_ID, ACTIVE_IND, NAME, ADDRESS_LINE_1, ADDRESS_LINE_2,
CITY, COUNTRY, CREDIT_CARD, CREDIT_LIMIT)
values (233, 'Y', 'Summit Energy', '733 Chesnutt Street', 'Suite 100', 'Eindhoven',
'Netherlands', '376733526924012', 529464);

insert into AP.VENDORS (VENDOR_ID, ACTIVE_IND, NAME, ADDRESS_LINE_1, CITY, COUNTRY,
CREDIT_CARD, CREDIT_LIMIT)
values (234, 'Y', 'Microsoft Corp.', '17 Ohita Street', 'Birmensdorf', 'Switzerland',
'377633413723886', 563995);

insert into AP.VENDORS (VENDOR_ID, ACTIVE_IND, NAME, ADDRESS_LINE_1, CITY, COUNTRY,
CREDIT_CARD, CREDIT_LIMIT)
values (235, 'Y', 'Telwares Communications', '56 Tate Drive', 'Erpe-Mere', 'Belgium',
'374133836623929', 556963);

insert into AP.VENDORS (VENDOR_ID, ACTIVE_IND, NAME, ADDRESS_LINE_1, CITY, COUNTRY,
CREDIT_CARD, CREDIT_LIMIT)
values (236, 'Y', 'Telechem International', '707 Lipnicki Ave', 'Gersthofen', 'Germany',
'379734355623746', 314982);

insert into AP.VENDORS (VENDOR_ID, ACTIVE_IND, NAME, ADDRESS_LINE_1, ADDRESS_LINE_2,
CITY, STATE, COUNTRY, CREDIT_CARD, CREDIT_LIMIT)
values (237, 'Y', 'Advanced Neuromodulation', '23 Sydney', 'Suite 100', 'Fountain
Hills', 'AZ', 'USA', '374034534222000', 549879);

insert into AP.VENDORS (VENDOR_ID, ACTIVE_IND, NAME, ADDRESS_LINE_1, CITY, COUNTRY,
CREDIT_CARD, CREDIT_LIMIT)
values (238, 'Y', 'L.E.M. Products', '68 Stanton Blvd', 'Moscow', 'Russia',
'379934286423082', 626670);

insert into AP.VENDORS (VENDOR_ID, ACTIVE_IND, NAME, ADDRESS_LINE_1, CITY, COUNTRY,
CREDIT_CARD, CREDIT_LIMIT)
values (239, 'Y', 'Commercial Energy of Montana', '73 Ifans Street', 'Hohenfels',
'Germany', '379633860223130', 464405);

insert into AP.VENDORS (VENDOR_ID, ACTIVE_IND, NAME, ADDRESS_LINE_1, CITY, COUNTRY,
CREDIT_CARD, CREDIT_LIMIT)
values (240, 'Y', 'WestNet Learning Technologies', '588 Varzea grande Road', 'San Jose',
'Costa Rica', '376233736522494', 206851);

insert into AP.VENDORS (VENDOR_ID, ACTIVE_IND, NAME, ADDRESS_LINE_1, CITY, STATE,
COUNTRY, CREDIT_CARD, CREDIT_LIMIT)
values (241, 'Y', 'Multimedia Live', '24 Bartlett Blvd', 'Annandale', 'PA', 'USA',
'376433949624613', 137745);

insert into AP.VENDORS (VENDOR_ID, ACTIVE_IND, NAME, ADDRESS_LINE_1, CITY, COUNTRY,
CREDIT_CARD, CREDIT_LIMIT)
values (242, 'Y', 'MRE Consulting', '61 McBride Street', 'North Sydney', 'Australia',
'379434138521693', 242956);

insert into AP.VENDORS (VENDOR_ID, ACTIVE_IND, NAME, ADDRESS_LINE_1, CITY, COUNTRY,
CREDIT_CARD, CREDIT_LIMIT)
values (243, 'Y', 'Adolph Coors Co.', '82 Maury Street', 'Mantova', 'Italy',
'373534645622503', 415050);

insert into AP.VENDORS (VENDOR_ID, ACTIVE_IND, NAME, ADDRESS_LINE_1, CITY, STATE,
COUNTRY, CREDIT_CARD, CREDIT_LIMIT)
```

```
values (244, 'Y', 'Meritage Technologies', '76 Syracuse Road', 'Bellevue', 'NE', 'USA',
'374333776324547', 462998);

insert into AP.VENDORS (VENDOR_ID, ACTIVE_IND, NAME, ADDRESS_LINE_1, ADDRESS_LINE_2,
CITY, STATE, COUNTRY, CREDIT_CARD, CREDIT_LIMIT)
values (245, 'Y', 'Computer Engineering Organization', '30 McConaughey Road', 'Suite
101', 'Englewood Cliffs', 'NJ', 'USA', '379333718323056', 221492);

insert into AP.VENDORS (VENDOR_ID, ACTIVE_IND, NAME, ADDRESS_LINE_1, CITY, COUNTRY,
CREDIT_CARD, CREDIT_LIMIT)
values (246, 'Y', 'In Zone', '91 Nelligan Ave', 'Oulu', 'Finland', '372634580924631',
588144);

insert into AP.VENDORS (VENDOR_ID, ACTIVE_IND, NAME, ADDRESS_LINE_1, CITY, STATE,
COUNTRY, CREDIT_CARD, CREDIT_LIMIT)
values (247, 'Y', 'Montpelier Plastics', '66 Weisz Blvd', 'Plymouth Meeting', 'PA',
'USA', '372733369423931', 92042);

insert into AP.VENDORS (VENDOR_ID, ACTIVE_IND, NAME, ADDRESS_LINE_1, CITY, COUNTRY,
CREDIT_CARD, CREDIT_LIMIT)
values (248, 'Y', 'Greenwich Technology Partners', '96 Carnes Street', 'Gothenburg',
'Sweden', '376334915624332', 107271);

insert into AP.VENDORS (VENDOR_ID, ACTIVE_IND, NAME, ADDRESS_LINE_1, CITY, COUNTRY,
CREDIT_CARD, CREDIT_LIMIT)
values (249, 'Y', 'TeleSynthesis', '740 Cromwell Drive', 'Yogyakarta', 'Indonesia',
'372933475824024', 417810);

insert into AP.VENDORS (VENDOR_ID, ACTIVE_IND, NAME, ADDRESS_LINE_1, CITY, STATE,
COUNTRY, CREDIT_CARD, CREDIT_LIMIT)
values (250, 'Y', 'Global Wireless Data', '41st Street', 'Spring Valley', 'NY', 'USA',
'377334935122741', 533887);

insert into AP.VENDORS (VENDOR_ID, ACTIVE_IND, NAME, ADDRESS_LINE_1, CITY, COUNTRY,
CREDIT_CARD, CREDIT_LIMIT)
values (251, 'Y', 'SCI', '92 Stockholm Drive', 'Helsingborg', 'Sweden',
'376933531021287', 545840);

insert into AP.VENDORS (VENDOR_ID, ACTIVE_IND, NAME, ADDRESS_LINE_1, ADDRESS_LINE_2,
CITY, STATE, COUNTRY, CREDIT_CARD, CREDIT_LIMIT)
values (252, 'Y', 'Travizon', '25 Storrington Road', 'Suite 201', 'Encinitas', 'CA',
'USA', '375534236922165', 343811);

insert into AP.VENDORS (VENDOR_ID, ACTIVE_IND, NAME, ADDRESS_LINE_1, CITY, COUNTRY,
CREDIT_CARD, CREDIT_LIMIT)
values (253, 'Y', 'Lynk Systems', '971 Hayes Road', 'Herne', 'Germany',
'377533883021372', 282257);

insert into AP.VENDORS (VENDOR_ID, ACTIVE_IND, NAME, ADDRESS_LINE_1, CITY, COUNTRY,
CREDIT_CARD, CREDIT_LIMIT)
values (254, 'Y', 'Progressive Medical', '43 Weisberg Road', 'Kungki', 'South Korea',
'378833369223581', 280256);

insert into AP.VENDORS (VENDOR_ID, ACTIVE_IND, NAME, ADDRESS_LINE_1, CITY, STATE,
COUNTRY, CREDIT_CARD, CREDIT_LIMIT)
values (255, 'Y', 'Greyhawk North America', '92nd Street', 'Mechanicsburg', 'PA', 'USA',
'375433761121016', 283276);

insert into AP.VENDORS (VENDOR_ID, ACTIVE_IND, NAME, ADDRESS_LINE_1, CITY, COUNTRY,
CREDIT_CARD, CREDIT_LIMIT)
values (256, 'Y', 'Laboratory Management Systems', '43 Curitiba Street', 'Farnham',
'United Kingdom', '377133791321782', 652779);

insert into AP.VENDORS (VENDOR_ID, ACTIVE_IND, NAME, ADDRESS_LINE_1, CITY, COUNTRY,
CREDIT_CARD, CREDIT_LIMIT)
values (257, 'Y', 'Fiberlink Communications', '83 Portsmouth Ave', 'Dortmund',
'Germany', '379334571023585', 256984);

insert into AP.VENDORS (VENDOR_ID, ACTIVE_IND, NAME, ADDRESS_LINE_1, CITY, STATE,
COUNTRY, CREDIT_CARD, CREDIT_LIMIT)
values (258, 'Y', 'Abatix', '25 Charlton Road', 'Valencia', 'CA', 'USA',
'372433268322733', 314357);

insert into AP.VENDORS (VENDOR_ID, ACTIVE_IND, NAME, ADDRESS_LINE_1, CITY, COUNTRY,
CREDIT_CARD, CREDIT_LIMIT)
values (259, 'Y', 'Kmart Corp.', '29 Macht Drive', 'Pecs', 'Hungary', '375334119224752',
49069);

insert into AP.VENDORS (VENDOR_ID, ACTIVE_IND, NAME, ADDRESS_LINE_1, CITY, COUNTRY,
CREDIT_CARD, CREDIT_LIMIT)
values (260, 'Y', 'CapTech Ventures', '52 Berkoff Drive', 'Maintenon', 'France',
'379934971221669', 303972);
```

```sql
insert into AP.VENDORS (VENDOR_ID, ACTIVE_IND, NAME, ADDRESS_LINE_1, CITY, STATE,
COUNTRY, CREDIT_CARD, CREDIT_LIMIT)
values (261, 'Y', 'Imaging Business Machines', '72 Assante Street', 'South Weber', 'UT',
'USA', '380133450522423', 256712);

insert into AP.VENDORS (VENDOR_ID, ACTIVE_IND, NAME, ADDRESS_LINE_1, CITY, COUNTRY,
CREDIT_CARD, CREDIT_LIMIT)
values (262, 'Y', 'Taycor Financial', '87 Ernie Street', 'Milton Keynes', 'United
Kingdom', '377234551723280', 440505);

insert into AP.VENDORS (VENDOR_ID, ACTIVE_IND, NAME, ADDRESS_LINE_1, CITY, COUNTRY,
CREDIT_CARD, CREDIT_LIMIT)
values (263, 'Y', 'eCopy', '831 Houston Ave', 'Sao paulo', 'Brazil', '377533694422951',
356514);

insert into AP.VENDORS (VENDOR_ID, ACTIVE_IND, NAME, ADDRESS_LINE_1, CITY, STATE,
COUNTRY, CREDIT_CARD, CREDIT_LIMIT)
values (264, 'Y', 'Biosite', '25 Ferraz  vasconcelos Drive', 'Lecanto', 'FL', 'USA',
'378334362822401', 211729);

COMMIT;

ALTER TABLE ap.invoices
    ENABLE CONSTRAINT invoices_vendor_fk;

-----
-- Load minimal test data into AP.INVOICES AND AP.INVOICE_ITEMS
-----
BEGIN
    ap.pkg_load_generator.RandomDML(25);
    COMMIT;
END;
/

ALTER TABLE ap.invoice_items
    ENABLE CONSTRAINT invoice_items_invoice_fk;

BEGIN
    DBMS_STATS.GATHER_SCHEMA_STATS(ownname => 'AP', cascade => TRUE);
END;
/
```

ABOUT THE AUTHORS

Charles Kim

Charles Kim is an Oracle ACE Director, Oracle Certified DBA, a Certified RAC Expert and Certified Exadata Implementation Specialist. Charles is also a VMware vExpert and a VMware Certified Professional. Charles specializes in complex data replication, Exadata, Virtualization and authored 10 books:

1. Oracle Database 11g New Features for DBA and Developers
2. Linux Recipes for Oracle DBAs
3. Oracle Data Guard 11g Handbook
4. Virtualizing Mission Critical Oracle Databases
5. Hadoop As A Service
6. Oracle ASM 12c Pocket Reference Guide
7. Expert Exadata Handbook
8. Solaris and Linux Recipes for DBAs
9. Oracle Cloud Pocket Solutions Guide
10. PDB ME to Oracle Cloud

Charles holds certifications in Oracle, VMware, Red Hat Linux and Microsoft, and has over 26 years of Oracle experience on mission and business critical databases. Charles presents regularly at local, regional, national, and international Oracle conferences including IOUG Collaborate, VMware World, and Oracle OpenWorld on topics of RAC, ASM, Linux Best Practices, Data Guard Best Practices, VMware virtualization, Oracle VMware virtualization, and 7×24 High Availability Considerations. Charles is the technical editor of the Automatic Storage Management book by Oracle Press and contributing author to the Database Cloud Storage: The Essential Guide to Oracle Automatic Storage Management book. Charles blogs at http://blog.dbaexpert.com.

Charles was the President of the Cloud SIG for the Independent Oracle User Group (IOUG) from 2014-2019. Charles's author page is located at: http://amazon.com/author/ckim/

His linkedin profile is: http://www.linkedin.com/in/chkim

His twitter tag is: @racdba

Jim Czuprynski

Jim Czuprynski has 35+ years of professional experience in his career in information technology, serving diverse roles at several Fortune 1000 companies before becoming an Oracle DBA in 2001. He was awarded the status of Oracle ACE Director in March 2014 and is a sought-after public speaker on Oracle Database technology features, presenting topics at Oracle OpenWorld, IOUG COLLABORATE, Hotsos Symposium, Oracle Technology Network ACE Tours, and Oracle User Group conferences around the world. Jim has authored over 100 articles focused on facets of Oracle Database administration to his credit since 2003 at **databasejournal.com** and **ioug.org**. He has also co-authored three books on Oracle database technology. His blog, **Generally ... It Depends** (http://jimczuprynski.wordpress.com), contains his regular observations on all things Oracle.

His linkedin profile is: http://www.linkedin.com/in/jczuprynski

His twitter tag is: @jimthewhyguy

Pini Dibask

Pini Dibask is an Oracle ACE and Oracle Certified Professional with more than 10 years of experience working as a Database Professional and as a Leader of Database Teams. He is currently a Senior Product Manager at Quest with global responsibility for Quest's flagship database performance monitoring portfolio. In his role, Pini is fueled by awesome customer experiences and passionate about building products people love that solve real-world customer pains.

Pini specializes in database performance tuning, high availability, data protection, and other core database areas. He is a frequent speaker at various conferences and database venues around the world including Oracle OpenWorld, IOUG Collaborate, RMOUG, DOAG, OUGN, and others. See his blog at: www.OracleDBPro.BlogSpot.com

His linkedin profile is: http://www.linkedin.com/in/pinidibask

His twitter tag is: @pini_dibask

A

ADO, 10, 68, 127, 129, 130, 131, 134, 135, 139, 141
Application Express, 35

B

Big Data, 5, 6

C

-c, 106, 145
capital expenses
  CapEx, 12
CDB, 9, 10, 48, 49, 50, 51, 52, 53, 54, 55, 56, 69, 70, 71, 72, 73, 74, 75, 81, 87, 88, 90, 91, 94, 96, 98, 99, 101, 102, 103, 105, 106, 113, 115, 118, 123, 124, 125, 142, 143, 144, 145, 146, 147, 148
CDB$ROOT, 10, 74, 142
Cloud, 1, 2, 3, 5, 9, 11, 12, 16, 17, 19, 20, 21, 22, 23, 25, 28, 29, 30, 32, 34, 35, 41, 45, 46, 77, 79, 101, 162

D

-d, 106
Data Guard, 5
Database In-Memory, 17
DBaaS, 9, 10, 13, 19, 22, 23, 26, 27, 28, 29, 30, 31, 34, 36, 41, 48, 52, 77, 81, 105
DBCA, 29, 48, 49, 50, 51
Dictionary Views, 10, 103
Dropped Pluggable Database, 10, 113

E

encryption keys, 51, 54, 55
Enterprise Manager, 35

F

FLASHBACK PLUGGABLE DATABASE, 105, 113, 116

H

Heat Maps, 10, 127, 136
Hot Migration, 81
Hybrid cloud
  hybrid cloud, 12

I

IaaS, 12
ILM, 10, 127, 130, 131, 132, 133, 134, 136, 137, 139, 140, 141
info, 6
Infrastructure-as-a-service
  IaaS, 12

K

keystores, 13, 51, 52, 54, 56, 73, 74

L

-l, 106, 145
Limiting IO, 10, 125

M

Memory Limits, 10, 126
Multitenancy, 17

N

NAS, 16
NFS, 16

O

operational expenses
  OpEx, 12
Oracle Virtual Machine, 17

P

PaaS, 12
PDB, 1, 2, 9, 10, 29, 40, 48, 49, 51, 55,
  56, 57, 58, 59, 69, 70, 71, 73, 74,
  75, 78, 81, 82, 83, 84, 85, 86, 87,
  88, 89, 90, 91, 93, 94, 95, 96, 98,
  99, 101, 102, 103, 105, 106, 107,
  108, 109, 110, 113, 114, 115, 116,
  117, 118, 120, 121, 122, 123, 124,
  125, 126, 127, 130, 142, 143, 144,
  145, 146, 147, 148, 149, 150, 151,
  162
PDB Lockdown Profile, 120, 121,
  122, 123
Platform as a service
  PaaS, 12
Point-In-Time Recovery, 10, 110
PROD_AP, 10, 58, 59, 68, 69, 70, 71,
  86, 87, 90, 93, 94, 95, 96, 97, 98,
  99, 127, 129, 130, 134, 151
Proxy PDBs, 10, 81, 101, 102, 103
PuTTY, 9, 36, 41, 42, 43, 44, 46, 48

R

RAC, 5

Refreshable PDBs, 10, 81, 93
Resource Governance, 10, 124
REST API, 9, 77, 79
RightScale, 11
RMAN, 10, 53, 105, 106, 107, 109,
  110, 111

S

SAN, 16
SHUTDOWN, 144
Software as a service
  SaaS, 12
STARTUP, 144, 148

T

TDE, 51, 52, 53, 54, 55, 56, 57, 58, 73,
  99
TWO_TASK, 10, 144

Z

-z (y)es, 106

Made in the USA
Columbia, SC
10 September 2019